Many Faces of Life Captured Through Poetry

Alvin Waite

World rights reserved. This book or any portion thereof may not be copied or reproduced in any form or manner whatever, except as provided by law, without the written permission of the publisher, except by a reviewer who may quote brief passages in a review.

The author assumes full responsibility for the accuracy of all facts and quotations as cited in this book. The opinions expressed in this book are the author's personal views and interpretations, and do not necessarily reflect those of the publisher.

This book is provided with the understanding that the publisher is not engaged in giving spiritual, legal, medical, or other professional advice. If authoritative advice is needed, the reader should seek the counsel of a competent professional.

Copyright © 2015 Alvin Waite

Copyright © 2015 Aspect Books

ISBN-13: 978-1-4796-0603-0 (Paperback)

ISBN-13: 978-1-4796-0604-7 (ePub)

ISBN-13: 978-1-4796-0605-4 (Mobi)

Library of Congress Control Number: 2015917061

To my mother Utilda; a tower of strength in my life,
&
To all who have experienced the many faces of life.

Table of Contents

Softer Side of Love	**9**	Spiritual Soldier	37
Oral Portraits	10	Corinthians' Charge	38
Man Up	10	Scriptures of Reassurance	38
Great Expectation	11	He Cares	39
Dear Woman	12	The Knock	40
Christmas List	12	God Says Yes	40
Woman's Worth	13	Christ in My Valley	41
She's Royal	14	Amazing Clay	42
His for Hers	15	Unseen Hands	43
Passion for Life	16	Hell's Highway	43
I Call You Beauty	17	Beware	44
A Woman's Heart	17		
Vague Beauty	18	**_History, Culture and Beliefs_**	**45**
Will It	19	Beliefs Kill, Beliefs Cure	46
Distant Pain	20	On the Other Side	47
That's All Right	20	Destination Canada	47
Love's Reciprocal	21	A Glimpse in the Past	49
Fade Away	22	Fun Cyaan Done	50
Flesh of my Flesh	22	Colours of Jamaica	50
Shallow	23	Image of Dancehall	51
Baby Mama	24	Gentleman	52
		Jamaica Will	53
Heroes Among Us	**25**	Foreigner	54
Heroes Among Us	26	Black Inventors	55
Super Dad	26	Nelson Mandela	56
Mother (To Mama with love)	27	Luther's Dream	57
A Mother's Love	28	Racial Barriers	58
On Mothers' Day	29	Mental Slavery	59
Diary of a Proud, Single Father	30	Oppression	59
Blessed Teacher	31	Self-Inferiority	60
Invaluable	31	My "N" Word	61
Report Card	32	Adrenaline Rush	61
		Wealth	62
On A Spiritual Note	**34**	Exposed	63
Monster Devil	35	Judas	63
The Prayer	35	Love	64
The True Light	36	Hate	65

My Brother's Keeper	66	My Shoes	89
Rare Friends	66	The FIFA Giant	90
Eulogy for the Late Self	67		
The Bully Coin	68	***Here & Now***	**92**
		Time	93
Dreams, Hopes & Aspirations	**70**	Age	93
Dreams and Aspirations	71	Generation of Nothing	94
We Are the World	72	Alcohol's Claws	95
Think Big	72	Time to Go	96
Gift of Love	73	Drugs	96
I Can	74	Different Me	97
Hidden In You	75	Moral Trauma	98
Still I Rise	75	I am Suicide	98
New Beginnings	76	Stony Land	99
Mistakes	77	Nothing	100
Dreams	77	Peaceful Sleep	100
Lost	78	Rain Amidst Sunshine	101
You Are	79	Technology	102
Past and Present	80	Dark Era	103
Rise	80	Never Felt My Pain	104
Greater Things	81	Overdue	104
I am a Multitude	82	Confused	105
Reflection	83	Life Cycle of a Hustler	106
Game Over	84	Midnight's Cry	107
Just Until	84	In the Streets	107
Go to the Ant	85	Heartless – Mindless	108
Education	86	My Purpose	109
Perfect Imperfections	86	Beauty and the Beast	110
Recovery	87	Poisoned Minds	110
Actions and Reactions	88	Hopeful Pain	111
Fix Your Roof	88	Appreciate It	112

Preface

An expressive art form, poetry brings one's inner thoughts, feelings, ideas and experiences alive, by the use of distinctive styles and rhythms. Poetry depends less on the nature, structure, and variation of language, sentence construction or paragraphs, and more on poetic organization.

Many Faces of Life Captured through Poetry, is an anthology of expressions through poetry which captures different aspects of life, both its acceptances and its challenges. Each poem is written with a target audience, and seeks to identify with them and their life's experiences; happiness, joys, fear, anger, grief and sufferings.

It seeks to give a sense of hope to those who feel hopeless, a sense of relief to those who are burdened and a sense of joy to those who seek happiness, all through the power of poetry.

I hope you will have many hours of enjoyment and an overall wonderful experience from indulging in the reading of these carefully selected poems written just for you.

Remember life is a precious gift. Life is short and time is luck. Live well, love much, and laugh more.

Alvin Waite

Softer Side of Love

Oral Portraits

I paint pictures with my words,
I create fine art.
I let you see my inner thoughts,
I take pride in my craft.

My words are my paint,
My canvas is your heart.
My tools create portrait of reality,
My visions on life I impart.

I speak what I see,
I let you see what I speak.
I make it clear as a glass,
I give you answers that you seek.

My time will soon expire,
My paintings will live on through time.
My messages will be remembered,
My will is to motivate you to shine.

I bring alive the visions,
My thoughts I now break free.
I live to give, I give to live,
My oral portraits I give to thee.

Man Up

Let her wake up to breakfast in bed, she would like that a lot,
Then wash all the dishes, don't leave her any dirty pots.
Help her wash the bathroom; it's only fair; you use it too.
Don't just leave all the household chores for your woman to do.

Remember that she is your partner; she is not your maid,
Who cleans up behind you without ever getting paid.
Remember that we are living in the modern age,
Gender roles don't exist; we have turned a brand new page.

Softer Side of Love

Help out around the house as much as you possibly can,
Doing household chores don't make you any less of a man.
Surprise her by doing the laundry, then fold the clothes when you are done,
And I can guarantee you that to her you'll be second to none.

Arrange a candle light dinner, prepare an exotic meal,
To you it might be nothing, but to her that's quite a big deal.
Give her a sensual massage, sweep her off her feet,
Play your notes right and she'll be marching to your beats.

Every woman is a mother's princess, and she should be a man's queen,
Once upon a time she stood out in your dream.
So don't just say I love you, let every action show,
Man up and be her hero, and on you her love she'll bestow.

Great Expectation

Genuine feeling of love and care
Radiance beaming from ear to ear
Emotions unlocked, no feeling of despair
Affections so pure; love extra-ordinaire
The depth of your heart can be seen from afar
Exceptional in every way; a character without mar
Xenodochial simply describes you.
Patient with everyone, no matter who
Each moment that passes, each moment we live
Create great memories; to you, my all I give
Treasures of happiness you hold deep inside
Abundant joys, and peace with you shall abide
Time has proven that our love is here to stay
Inspired by your virtue, from you I'll never stray
Ordinary creature with extra ordinary effects
Nurture or nature; woman you are the best.

Dear Woman

I don't look at your makeup, nor do I look at your bangles and chains,
Your short dress doesn't impress me, it doesn't ignite any flames.
I see so many piercings, it's as if you are made of steel,
What impresses me is a woman that is one hundred percent real.

Her character doesn't have to be flawless, but virtue must be seen,
A woman who isn't virtuous could never be my queen.
Her high confidence is shown by the way she carries herself,
She doesn't have her assets on display like products on a shelf.

You may think that exposing your body is an act of liberation,
But it isn't when your intention is to intensify flirtation.
Why equate control of your body with nudity and sexual suggestiveness?
Doesn't that counteract with feminism causing it to lose its effectiveness?

Dear woman, there's more power in decency than there is in nudity,
You don't have to expose your assets; it's your character that shows
    true beauty.
It doesn't show womanism, it shows that you are insecure,
Don't use your body as a public spectacle … you are worth much more.

Don't just be a woman, be a lady full of grace,
Command respect from everyone, elevate yourself to a higher place.
Aim to be extra-ordinary, let the imagination of the onlookers work,
Set positive modesty standards, remember … decency doesn't hurt.

Christmas List

Every woman has a Christmas list; she made it from early fall,
She won't tell you about it but she expects you to know it all.
A man will never understand fully how a woman operates,
But for all the trouble that we go through… her happiness compensates.

If you want to ensure that you have a very merry Christmas,
Which includes very little arguments and very little fuss,
There are a few things that I would recommend that you do,

To ensure that the season isn't just merry, but intimate too.

First and foremost get her some special gifts,
You don't really have to know what's on her Christmas list.
Fragrances are a must, with that you can never go wrong,
And when presenting it to her, sing her a love song.

Get her some underwear; that gesture has powerful effects,
She'll giggle and blush when she receives it, and you know what will come next.
Pay attention to details; make sure the colour and size are just right,
You will be a romantic giant in your woman's sight.

She will enjoy a necklace; make sure that it's not fake,
It might irritate her skin and causes both of you much ache.
A spa date can be lovely; the relaxation will do her well,
Let her see the effort you make and she'll be like a damsel under your spell.

The most important thing to note even before you start,
Whatever gift you can afford should be coming straight from the heart.
Don't overspend …just make sure it screams "I care"
You'll have a merry intimate Christmas, so you better be prepared.

Woman's Worth

A woman is more precious than diamonds or pearls,
She holds more value than anything in this world.
She's a priceless gift taken from the rib of man,
But without her, life really wouldn't have begun.

She is the forefront of God's master plan.
When a man will quit, she will firmly stand,
When he gives up, she will hold his hand,
What a woman can tolerate, a man can never withstand.

A woman's worth goes far beyond physical appearance.
We place value on face, ignoring her brilliance,

Treating her like an object, not recognizing her importance.
We treat her as if she is of no significance.

The colour of her skin doesn't matter; neither does the texture of her hair,
Her weight or height shouldn't be a factor; neither should the clothes that she wears.
We shouldn't judge her by our objective standards, to her that's not quite fair.
Because of our subjective reasoning, we ignorantly bring many women to tears.

We focus on appearance but ignore the most important part,
We compliment her ravishing appearance; but fail to look at her loving heart.
We listen to the way she speaks, we even judge her by the way she walks,
We are quick to judge her, pointing out all her flaws.

She is compassionate, caring, loving and kind,
She is the opposite of man, she was made refined.
Our shallowness has prevented us from seeing a woman's true worth,
How often do we stop to think about her true purpose on this earth?

She's Royal

He adores his children, yet still he calls their mother fat,
He looks at her with disgust wishing her stomach was still flat.
He no longer admires her, this virtuous woman he ignores,
Just because her figure has being distorted, she isn't sexy to him as before.

He gets upset with her, when at nights she unconsciously snuffle,
But her days are very hectic and her chores she cannot reshuffle.
He comes home daily to a clean house and a warm cooked meal,
But still he finds reasons to complain, ignoring how she feels.

His clothes for work are pressed and his shirts are folded neat,
And when he complains of a long hard day she humbly rubs his feet.
Yet still he doesn't appreciate her, he cannot see her worth,
He can't even comprehend how much to a woman that hurts.

She tries her best to please him, fearing for the worst,
But still he puts her last, everything else he puts first.
She knows in her heart that she's a special human being,
In the sight of God she's royal, and to the right man she's a queen.

He'd better starts appreciating her; he needs to treat her well,
Love her like he has never loved her before, or he'll have a sad story to tell.
Compliment her when she wakes and before she goes to sleep,
Give her reassuring kisses and that's a woman that he'll forever keep.

If she walks out the door she's never going to return,
She'll pack her stuff and leave his sorrowful heart to burn.
She'll go in search of happiness, and she will find it too,
She'll rise above his level, leaving him sad, lonely and confused.

His for Hers

He uses his life to make hers better,
This is the true meaning of what it means to be a partner.
She'll use her life to compliment his ways,
So he'll have peaceful nights and fruitful days.

He's willing to suffer so she doesn't hurt,
He'll finish last so she can finish first,
She's willing to hurt just to ease his pains,
She'll be submissive, allowing his ego to reign.

He'll starve himself to make sure that she eats,
He'll give her the most and happily takes the least.
She'll take what she's given and it will multiply,
Many wants for herself she will deny.

He'll search for water so she doesn't thirst,
He'll give her the best and humbly takes the worst.
She'll quench her thirst with the water he brings,
Then soothes his spirit with the songs that she sings.

He'll learn to build a house so she can have shelter,
He'll endanger his life just to be her protector.
She'll work very hard to turn the house into a home,
Filled with love and dreams, nothing to bemoan.

Him for her, her for him,
When true love shines it can never go dim.
He's her diamond, she's his pearl,
Together they are each other's world.

Passion for Life

I don't have all the things that I want, but I have everything that I need,
I have you in my life so I feel blessed, well blessed indeed.
I may not be very wealthy, but I'm rich as one can be,
I can feel your gentle touch and your beautiful face I can see.

Even when the time is cold I'm kept warm by your embrace,
No matter how old we grow your love can never be replaced.
You are my passion for life, until death do us part,
I'll be forever by your side; you hold the keys to my heart.

I don't complain about the "have nots", I'm thankful for what I've got,
Too many blessings to be ungrateful, I've been given a whole lot.
When I think about my life and the joys that you bring,
All the love that you give, it makes the bells in my heart ring.

You bring balance to my life, you make it complete,
The outpouring of your amazing love makes me feel replete.
You have made me who I am; you have showed me that I can,
You have helped me up to stand, showing me that I'm greater than.

I am spell bound, I am walking tall,
You have me captivated, you have me enthralled.
You have started in me a very intense and uncontrollable fire,
You are at the forefront of all my desires.

I Call You Beauty

You are skilfully carved into a voluptuous being,
The most beautiful woman I have ever seen.
The way your body curves in style,
Is perfectly matched with your beautiful smile.

Your lips are tantalizing, I love how they taste,
I am well pleased to stare in your perfectly constructed face.
Your beatific expression makes me feel warm,
I know you and I can easily weather any storm.

When you smile I'm taken away,
You enlighten my nights, you brighten my days.
Through my eyes you are perfect in every single way.
The feeling that you give me, words cannot say … you simply take my breath away.

The little things you do make me realize
That awesome women exists, I don't have to fantasize.
Perfection isn't just found in unrealistic dreams,
You are a living fact and I do believe.

You are the epitome of what a lady should be,
The most virtuous woman one can ever see.
You never cease to amaze me, the innocence of you;
Pure, wholesome, down to earth, I see love that's really true.

You are blest with a gift that has been given to just a few,
A gift that many persons can never construe;
Intelligence beyond comparison, beauty second to none,
Character which is unmatched, you cannot be outdone.

A Woman's Heart

There's nothing more forgiving than a woman's heart,
She'd score 9.9 if there was a "forgiving hearts' chart."
She's very understanding and will tolerate much,
All the turmoil that comes with men she'll put up with such.
That's the strength and power of a woman's heart.

She'll give you enough chances to straighten yourself out,
She'll help you with the things that you don't know much about.
Her resilience will shock you; don't expect an ignominious retreat,
She is never oblivious, and will not accept an easy defeat.
That's the perseverance and prowess of a woman's heart.

Passionate, gentle, caring and kind,
The affection she gives will blow your mind.
But never take her heart, love or kindness for granted,
It can turn into "fire of fury," especially if she feels overly disrespected.
That's the beauty and the beast of a woman's heart.

Don't take her kindness or sweetness for weakness,
Even when full of anger she'll display much meekness.
Remember hell knows no fury like a woman's scorn,
It's like getting caught between a raging bull's horns.
That's the hate and disdain of a woman's heart.

If she means to spite you, suffer you must,
She'll say I love you this moment, next moment she'll create a fuss.
There's nothing worse than a woman's love turned into hate,
You'll never win her back no matter how much you debate.
Never take slightly the powers of a woman's heart.

Vague Beauty

She is the definition of gorgeous; her beauty is second to none,
When she smiles the place radiantly lights up like the sun.
Her teeth are white and are perfectly lined in place,
Her lips are beautifully curved; they complement her face.

She's well educated and quite eloquent in speech,
Lessons in grammar she can always teach.
When she walks she'll amaze you, she takes pride in the steps she makes,
She'll have you hypnotized, your breath she'll take away.

Her shoulders wide, she walks like a queen,
She's really a picture to look at, - most beautiful girl you've ever seen.
Under that beautiful smile and that perfect skin,
Is a woman who is dim, one that is ugly as sin.

She sports a beautiful face which hides an ugly character,
That's like a lamb with meek appearance that has the heart of a tiger.
Perfect appearance, extra-ordinary physique,
Impeccable smile that will make you weak.

She idolizes vanity, she's completely vague,
To satisfy her materialistic needs, she'll do whatever it takes.
She works the streets at nights, and takes her rest during the day,
She is well skilled in her profession; she has led many men astray.

Her house is always busy, many men come and go,
This woman is a prostitute, but looking at her you wouldn't know.
So the next time you see a woman, get to know her well,
Don't get distracted by her ravishing looks or her intoxicating smell.

Will It

Will it be on the beach or will it be in the park?
Will the sun be up or will it be dark?
Will the stars be shining in the sky?
Will the beautiful moon shows its big bright smile?

Will we be warm or will we be cold?
I promise I won't wait until you get old,
We'll be able to sit and enjoy our story being told,
Of when I went down on my knees
And ask the most beautiful woman in this world to marry me.

Distant Pain

Distance, oh distance! Why keep us apart?

You are sad when I'm lonely; I'm lonely when you are sad.
I reach out for you to hold me, but I can't find your hands.

Our love is cheated by distance, how far away we are,
I've tried so many times to wish upon a star,
That when I whisper your name, you'll come running in my arms.

O distance why art thou so cruel? You have separated me from my love,
I thought you wouldn't have prevailed, and I would have been reunited
    with my dove.
I have given her all my love, and she has given me all her heart,
Distance, oh distance! Why keep us apart?

That's All Right

Waking up beside you, that's alright,
Your kisses on my lips, tastes just right.
You are perfect for me and that's so right,
I'll follow beside you, left or right.

I can listen to your "I love you" all day and night.
I need you to be around, always in sight.
Situation gets tough, sometimes they get tight,
But to make you comfortable, I'll forever fight.

Even if I have to work from dust till dawn,
I'll give you that white picket fence and perfect lawn.
The thought of your hugs keeps me warm,
As long as I'm with you we can weather any storm.

Softer Side of Love

If I could draw my love it would be a picture deemed perfect,
Then I'd seal it with a kiss, and give it much respect.
I'll forever try to impress you like the first day we met.
The love I hold for you can only be cancelled by death

You are like a best kept secret, you deserve my all,
When I'm with you, I walk tall.
You make loving you easy, although love is hard,
For you I will walk the longest yard.

Love's Reciprocal

I give you take, I take you give,
In happiness forever we both shall live.
Many sacrifices we have made,
Great rewards we have gained,
Love's reciprocal.

Together we speak, together we listen,
From each other we have learnt many great lessons.
Mutual respect in every aspect,
Working together to ensure happiness,
Love's reciprocal.

Tolerance and understanding has made us unite,
Living in harmony and with sincerity has been our delight.
Certain principles and values together we have shared,
Achieving great happiness, showing each other we care.
Love's reciprocal.

Our love is more like a delicate plant; we have to nurture it well,
So it can grow strong and old and in our hearts continually dwell.
We are not perfect but our love can achieve perfection,
To each other we have shown maximum affection,
Love's Reciprocal.

I for you, you for me,
This love can be whatever we want it to be.
Dedication and respect are the keys to achieve what we seek,
Helping our love to grow stronger, never going weak.
Love's reciprocal, keeping it real.

Fade Away

Fade away, I don't want this love to fade away,
Too much heartache, too many cries, too many sad and lonely nights.
Fade away, please love don't fade away,
Too many tears fall from my eyes, too much pain in saying goodbye.

Fade away, if this love ever fades away,
I'll be broken, I'll be torn, I'll be left to constantly mourn.
Fade away, I have to stop this love from fade away,
Please don't sink me in the deep, do not leave me here to weep.

Fade away, please don't let our love fade away,
Let's give our love a chance to live; let's give love another day.
Fade away, I don't want this love to fade away,
Too much heartache, too many cries, too many sad and lonely nights.

Flesh of my Flesh

We fuss, we fight, we curse, we cry,
To hurt each other with words we try.
We harden our hearts to the feelings of the other,
Our words are cold and sharp when they battle together.

Once our words danced happily like fairies in the sky,
Now they battle like enemies wanting each other to die.
Once our tongues met only when sweet kisses were due,
Now they meet like a cock fight; each other to subdue.

We make perfect, throwing words that cut emotions like a sword,
Whatever words of peace are exchanged is flatter than a piece of board.
Our hearts left torn; the effects of thoughtless, poisonous utterances,
Leaving scars that are deep, simply because we cannot settle
　our differences.

But behind those bitter words does a love still exist?
Does the heart still pump emotions that the mind tries to resist?
It's never too late for love to find its way home,
Flesh of my flesh, bone of my bone.

Shallow

Thoughts are shallow, they are without depth,
The things that you utter, your mind they should not have left.
You seem to be a quick utterer, but a very slow contemplator,
Eager to voice your opinions which are like blank pieces of paper.

You are quite confident when you speak; you articulate your words well,
But the things you vocalize should be better left unsaid.
Sometimes it's best to ponder before you actually speak,
As eloquent as you are, your arguments are quite weak.

What goes on in that mind of yours, everybody knows,
Whatever your words fail to express, your actions surely shows.
Your attitude is a reflection of the inner you,
The things that you say are similar to the things that you do.

You may enunciate your words well; you may be eloquent when you speak,
When you open your mouth you attract the attention that you seek.
People look at you in awe, they are amazed by the things you say,
To you it makes perfect sense, to others you are the joke of the day.

A slow thinker and a fast utterer is always seen as unwise,
So if you are laughed at when you speak, don't be surprised.
You are not less smart if at times you have nothing to say,
Keep your thoughts in your head, sometimes that's where they are
　meant to stay.

Baby Mama

We are not together … She is not my lover,
I must have been blind not to see her other side.
I care about her because she's my baby's mother,
But with this shallow minded woman I just could not abide.

This woman is quite ratchet, I think she is insane,
She is physically refined, but she has lost her mind.
She curses for every reason, and throw blows that causes pain,
She'll stab you with harsh words that are very unkind.

She is extremely curvaceous and very pleasing to the eyes,
The way she flaunts her assets will drive any man wild.
She is a beautiful tigress hidden in a fairies disguise,
It's hard to believe this uncultured woman is the mother of my child.

She provokes every woman that I talk with; she drives them far away,
She is on a mission to break me, hoping to catch me when I fall.
But this old fool has learnt his lesson; as far away from her I'll stay,
There is no rekindling for these dead flames; she no longer has me enthrall.

Respect the boundaries I ask her please, there's a line she must not cross,
In her life I am just our baby's dad, and that's all I will ever be.
Even though you have given me a priceless gift, this I say with no remorse,
You are not the woman for me; stay away from my heart is my decree.

*Heroes
Among
Us*

Heroes Among Us

There are heroes among us, some we will never know,
These names will never be called, or on them honour will never
 be bestowed.
They will never make the headlines or become a household name,
These are our unsung heroes, who don't seek glory or fame.

The teacher who patiently gives her students tender love and care,
And the little child who humbly takes his meagre lunch and share.
The police officer who bravely patrols the dangerous streets at nights,
And the young lad who encourages his peers to walk away from a fight.

The child who rescues the neighbour's cat, showing that he is brave,
And the preacher who preaches with all his might; so many souls he save.
The doctors, nurses, farmers and fire-fighters too,
Without their dedicated services, we simply cannot do.

The mothers and fathers who sacrifice so much,
Who never fail to give their children that very special touch,
They nurture them throughout their many different life stages,
If they should write a book, it would contain countless pages.

To all our unsung heroes, we pay homage to you dear,
Some of you have worked so hard, sacrificing blood, sweat and tears.
You have made your contribution; on us you have left your mark,
To our unsung heroes, your names are engraved on someone's heart.

Super Dad

I never knew my father; I heard he was quite a man,
He had great physical appearance, tall, robust and strong.
He was the village's Physician, Tailor and Preacher too,
My father, my unsung hero; there was nothing he couldn't do.

A farmer by profession, he planted lots of crops,
He also was an entrepreneur; he owned the village's only shop.

Heroes Among Us

He was very resourceful; he knew his medicine well,
The villagers all looked up to him, their lives he somehow impelled.

He was the captain of the cricket team; they were unbeaten in every match,
Every man wanted to be like him; to the women he was quite the catch.
He wasn't afraid to show the world how valiant he could be,
For wherever there was a problem to be solved, his presence you would see.

He spoke at every function; he was quite eloquent in speech,
He always had encouraging words to give to whomever he would preach.
He wasn't afraid to correct you when you mispronounced your words,
Your grammar had to be perfect when with him you conversed.

He took pride in his appearance; he was a well-groomed man,
Wherever he went he walked tall, a stalwart of the land.
He taught positive values and attitudes to all who listened to him,
He encouraged all to show gratitude for every little thing.

With all these gifts he showed humility, a humble man he was,
He knew all too well he was nothing without the Lord above.
He prayed earnestly like Daniel, He exercised patience like Job,
His wisdom was great like Solomon, and like Abraham he grew old.

Mother (*To Mama with love*)

There are not enough adjectives to describe my mother,
A woman full of virtue who was peculiar when choosing my father.
She is characterized by selflessness, gentility and humility,
She is always optimistic, always full of positivity.

She never utters a doubtful word,
A more virtuous woman is unheard.
She is an upstanding woman, who is fare in all her doings,
Happiness and love is what she is pursuing.

A godly and spiritual woman my mom is indeed,
Daily the Scriptures she fervently reads.
She extends her hands to the needy and opens her arms to the poor,
Never would she turn a person in need away from her door.

Her family can be confident in her; she never lets them down,
No matter the situation, she never wears a frown.
She's not impetuous, scatterbrained or unpredictable,
Mama is simply delightful, mama is unforgettable.

She speaks with wisdom and faithful instructions are on her tongue,
She will guide you on the right path whether old or young.
Mama, many women are seen as noble, but you surpass them all,
Many good deeds you have done, so many we can't recall.

You are clothed with integrity, strength and dignity,
You have proven your worth and versatility continually.
An outstanding example of a woman of God's own heart,
You are the woman of proverbs thirty first, in whole, not in part.

Mama we call you blessed, you have helped us to bring out our best,
You are a heroine in our eyes, no other mother can contest.
You are our super woman; we love and adore you so dear,
Mama, we are confident that you will one day rest in God's care.

A Mother's Love

A mother's unconditional love for her child knows no ends,
It is without boundaries and never broken, no matter how it bends.

It acts as a shelter during life's most violent storms,
It challenges every trend and breaks every norm.

It's a light that guides you through the darkest, most frightening nights,
And turns every horrifying shadow into bright, shining sights.

A mother's love generates warmth like the giant stars of the sky,
When this love is unleashed, it can never go awry.

It is a full body armour with the aim to protect,
Mother's love cushions and embodies you just like a bird's nest.

A mother's love never fails, no matter the hardships it face,
It flourishes with much affection and is always full of grace.

Only a mother can really explain the depth of a mother's love,
Which extends as deep as the depth of the earth and as high as the heavens above.

Thank you mother for a love that knows no end,
You have been more than a mother, you have been a best friend.

On Mothers' Day

Special describes that which is great,
Awesome beings God did create,
Mothers fit the definition of "SPECIAL" just right,
In this dark world, mothers shine so bright.

When we think of the great things we wouldn't have known without you,
All the lessons that you have taught us, morals and values so true,
We realize that you were specially designed in God's great plan.
So many things that others cannot do, you mother surely can.

Mother's dream for their children and help to push them to the sky,
They are always there to wipe the tears from their children's eyes.
They encourage and motivate the dads to push forward from day to day,
We're blessed to have God-fearing mothers, who on their knees they'll pray.

We love you mothers and we just want you to know,
Today is your day, and on you our love we humbly bestow.
We pray God's richest blessing on you from now until,
Happy mother's day, and we hope your wishes God will fulfill.

Diary of a Proud, Single Father

I do it for my son, who cannot do it for himself,
It's not his duty to put food on the cupboard shelf.
I proudly do it on my own; I am the sole provider,
This is the diary of a proud, single Father.

I wake up at the crack of dawn,
I stretch, I smile, I pray, I yawn.
I attend to the duties of the man in the yard,
Something that I know every real man look towards.

My boy has his own duties as a discipline child,
He isn't allowed to be loose or to run in the streets wild.
After we eat, we conduct worship and then we pray,
I try to give my boy a prayerful start to an untried day.

Prayer gives me the strength that I need to be strong,
To toil and labour on the farm all day long.
Whether the sun is scorching hot or there's falling of torrential rains,
I labour with love for my boy, knowing it will not go in vain.

I get home before my son; I greet him at the gate,
He knows too well to be home on time and he is never late.
We both do our evening chores, and then dinner is served,
My boy is worth my sacrifice and my best is what he deserves.

Evening worship is important; we use it to close the day,
Thanking God for protecting us from harms that came our way.
Homework and study must be done before going to bed,
I ensure that my boy is physically, spiritually and academically fed.

I am indeed proud but I do not brag or boast,
Instead I use our situation to help him to accomplish the most.
I try to raise a gentleman in the absence of a mother,
I am indeed a very blessed, proud single father.

Blessed Teacher

Whether it's cleaning the mucus from a child's messy nose,
Or wiping the flow of blood from a child's cut toe.
Settling a simple dispute or parting a severe fight,
Or just helping a child with the flying of a kite.

Comforting a child who bruises his knees,
Or encouraging them to wash their hands after they pee.
Wiping the sobbing tears of a child who cries,
Or congratulating a defiant child who finally tries.

Sharing lunch with a helpless, hungry child,
Or unlocking emotions that a child hides.
Diagnosing the cause of a child's hurt or pains,
They do these because of love, not financial gains.

Watching the smile of a child that has just learnt to read,
Or helping an entire family with their social needs.
A teacher nurtures a room full of children every single day,
They monitor their development in every single way.

They feed, they preach, they lead, they teach,
Helping children to set goals that they can reach.
A teacher is a mother, a father, and caregiver too,
They do what police, nurses, judges and social workers do.

Living the life of a teacher is not an easy task,
Their job description is amazingly vast.
So the next time you see a teacher show him or her respect,
In every nation their work has much effect.

Invaluable

The world depends on farming, so why are farmers poor?
That sector provides our greatest need; it is needed in galore.

Every meal we eat to God we should say thanks,
For giving farmers the strength to toil and the ability to use their hands.

Teachers shape the future, why are they underpaid?
They are treated with scant regard, but on them high responsibilities are laid.
They need motivation to carry on their tremendous task,
So for better wages and conditions, they shouldn't even have to ask.

Policemen put their lives on the line, sometimes they end up traumatized,
And the way they are treated by the public, makes them become demoralized.
They should be greatly compensated for their hard work and distress,
So they can provide for their family and give them the best.

Doctors and nurses are always busy saving precious lives,
So they shouldn't have to protest for wage increase to live a better life.
Civil servants are the driving force behind any nation's success,
They should be treated with love and utmost respect.

For their invaluable service they can never be really compensated,
So we should do our part to make them feel appreciated.

Report Card

My child, my child I'm taking you to school,
Why are your grades so low? I haven't raised a fool.
You were an "A" student, now your grades are at naught,
What is your teacher doing, hasn't he taught?

Hurry my child, hurry! You know I love to be on time,
I will not accept a report card like this for any child of mine.
Your teacher has lost his mind; he has some explaining to do,
I need to know why on earth he has issued these grades to you.

Good morning teacher, I am Jane, and this is my child Sue,
I'm not pleased with her report card, that's why I've come to see you.

After one term in your class, this is all she has to show,
She hasn't shown any progress … she did not grow.

So please tell me, dear teacher, why are her grades so low,
You can understand my concerns as a parent, I really want to know.
Dear teacher, her poor performance reflects your inability to teach,
Anyway, I'm here to get an explanation, I'm not here to preach.

Dear parent it's nice to finally meet you, this meeting is long overdue,
I must say that is has been quite a pleasure to teach your child Sue.
I understand your concerns, and as a parent it shows that you care,
But as her teacher I also have some concerns, so please allow me to share.

You never attend any meetings, so you don't know what's going on,
Right throughout the school day, all Sue does is yawn.
She comes to school very tired; sleepiness in her eyes,
So when she doesn't retain anything taught, I am far from surprised.

She complains about been hungry from as early as 10:00 a.m.,
The noises her stomach makes in the class will one day create mayhem.
It really makes me wonder what's going on at home,
Does she have a mother there, or does she live alone.

She doesn't do assignments, and at home she doesn't take up a book,
And all these little drawbacks are things that you cannot overlook.
There has to be some balance between home and school,
This will make her grades improve, because I haven't taught a fool.

*On
A
Spiritual
Note*

Monster Devil

You told me that I was nothing and I actually believed,
You said many blessings you had to give and I had much to receive.
From the day I met you, nothing good about you I perceived,
I shouldn't have allowed myself to be foolishly deceived.

You took me down a path that led to self-destruction,
You tricked me into believing that for me there was no reconstruction.
You told me that my life was worthless and there was no restitution,
And it was best for me to do a self-termination.

You dragged me at your feet; I thought I was dead,
So many lies you filled up in my poor, confused head.
I needed to be showed love but you abused me instead,
You went back on every single word that you boldly said.

You have offered me nothing but pain, shame and disgrace,
But now I shun the very appearance of your face.
Your sweet lies and empty promises I never want to taste,
In my life, monster devil, you have no more place.

The Prayer

Dear Lord, I recognize thee as my personal saviour from sin,
The one with the power to cleanse me within.
The all-powerful, all mighty, master of the earth,
Who knelt, and with love, moulded man from just dirt.
Your power manifests itself through this vast universe,
That is why I will never cease to put everything last and put you first.

Holy of Holies, I thank you for this day,
I thank you for the ability and the privilege to pray.
Thanks for opening my eyes showing me a clear path,
And for showing me love even when I deserved your wrath.
I'll forever stay under your wings; I want to feel your warmth.

Father, keep me safe from my enemies, protect me from my friends,
They've proven to be untrustworthy time and time again.
Help me to show them kindness, but give me strength for self-defence,
Give me clear vision to recognize those who love me in pretence.

I plead with thee to give me a loving and forgiving heart,
It's hard to love my enemies, but I'm willing to make a start.
I have a responsibility; help me to play my part.

Forgive me of my transgressions, each day they multiply,
I'm tired of sinning; only you I want to satisfy.

Your name I magnify, only you I glorify.

The True Light

Jesus is the epitome of what a man should be,
He saw every man as His brother, no matter race, colour or creed.
No matter your stance in life, no matter your belief,
He offered much assurance, and gave much relief.

He didn't believe in envy, He didn't believe in greed,
He didn't believe in stealing, but He didn't hate the thief.
In fact He even assured one, in paradise you shall be with me.
He gave eternal hope to a thief, who, spiritually could not see.

He loved the small children, He taught them love and peace,
He taught that envy, hate and greed are traits that we should cease.
He never turned a blind eye to anyone in need,
It was always His pleasure to do a good deed.

He was always a very kind man; He has lots of riches in store,
And today He is knocking, wanting to enter through your heart's door.
He doesn't want to bother you, or interrupt your busy life,
He just wants to help you to be more like Jesus Christ.

He doesn't owe us any favour; it's ok for us to choose,
But be careful of the choice you make, you might be the one to lose.
He sees things that we can't see; He knows our every move,
We can chose eternal life or chose to be eternally doomed.

Leave space for Jesus in your life, give him enough room.
He wants to be our closest friend, remember He is coming soon.
Don't miss out on Glory land, it's there for you and me,
Let's purpose in our hearts that Heaven is where we'll be.

Spiritual Soldier

I'm a different kind of soldier battling a different kind of war,
Having different kinds of enemies giving me different types of scars.
I'm in a different type of army, fighting a different type of fight,
Using different types of weapons, seeing a different victory in sight.

My armor is unique, it offers me full protection,
I'm able to withstand any ammunition the enemy hurls in my direction.
My battle isn't normal, it certainly isn't carnal,
This spiritual warfare may be subliminal, but it is certainly critical.

I'm wearing the hardest helmet; it's the helmet of salvation,
It protects me from the enemy's most dangerous ammunitions.
The breast plate of righteousness is solid as can be,
The enemy's sword and spear can never pierce me.

My waist is girded with the belt of truth,
It keeps me standing upright, whether things are rough or smooth.
I can both attack and defend with the sword of the spirit,
Be sure to be armed every second of every minute.

The shield of faith helps me to step up and step out,
I can go fourth without having a shadow of a doubt-
That His protection is real, I abide safely under His wings,
I can fight this battle without fearing anything.

I can shout for joy, songs of praises I can sing,
He is helping me fight my battles; I know I am going to win.
His tender, loving and merciful hands
Are keeping me safe from the devil's evil plan.

Corinthians' Charge

Love is patient, love is kind,
That heart of love I'm trying to find.
Love does not anger nor does it boast,
A love like that I want the most

Love is not arrogant nor is it rude,
A love like that needs a heart that isn't crude.
Love does not insist in its own selfish way,
It is dependent on the Lord, day by day.

Love is neither irritable nor resentful,
But shows in many ways that it is very merciful.
Love does not rejoice in anything evil,
It rejoices in the Lord and rejects the devil.

Love bears, believes, hopes and endures all things,
It is a virtue endorsed by the Lord of Lords, our King of Kings.
Prophecy, tongue and knowledge will cease and vanish away,
But real, pure, true love will never fade.

Scriptures of Reassurance

On my pitiful afflicted bed,
A message of hope God tried to extend,
Turn to Mathew 21 verse 22 He said.

If you still lack faith,
Read Mathew 7 verse 7 and 8.

On A Spiritual Note

Prayer is not just a routine
Consider Saint John 14 verses 13 to14.

If you want miracles to be seen,
Study James 5 verses 13 to 16.

Don't be selfish, intercede for everyone,
That's what it says in 1 Timothy 2 verse 1.

If you have problems for Him to fix,
Don't hesitate, read Philippians 4 verse 6.

He Cares

What do you do when life offers you no comfort?
And you have become so blind you have lost sight of the Comforter?
What do you do when life doesn't smile at you again?
And all the cares of life threatens to drive you insane?

You find a very tranquil place to stop and meditate for a while,
You tell yourself, no matter what, I am going to continually smile.
You take a moment to talk with God and tell Him all your fears,
He will use His gentle hands to wipe away your tears.

What do you do when you have lost all your joys?
And the things you once took pride in you no longer enjoy?
What do you do when the hills become too steep to climb?
Or the rivers you once crossed now become too wide?

You take a moment to reflect on all the blessings God has bestowed,
You take the time to talk to Him, even though He already knows.
He'll allow, in your life, unimaginable abundance of joy to flow,
He'll make the darkness in your life be transformed to a heavenly glow.

There has never been a whisper too silent for Him to hear,
Or a burden that exists, too heavy for Him to bear.

There has never been a tear that He doesn't understand,
He'll take you through it all, He has unchanging hands.

Don't allow yourself to be battered by life's terrible, raging storm,
Invite Jesus in your boat, He can keep the angry winds calm.
Behind every dark cloud, He is the silver lining.
Remember He is never late; He has perfect timing.

The Knock

Behold, He stands at the door and knocks – He knocks,
Even when our heart's door is hard as rock– He knocks.

We stray far away from His flock, He searches for us – and He knocks.
We harden our hearts and reject His call – still He knocks.

He lifts us up, we continue to fall – but He knocks,
We fail to recognize Him as Lord of All– still He Knocks.

Our hearts are desperately wicked and full of evil- but He knocks,
We shun the Lord but walks with the devil – still He knocks.

We are like little spiritual rebels,
How long will it take us to trust God and be settled?

How long will you make our Lord wait?
Open your heart's door before it is eternally too late.

God Says Yes

God says yes when the devil says no,
When the devil tries to stop you, God says go.
God showers you with blessings while the devil casts curse,
God offers the best but the devil gives the worst.

The light of love is Jesus, Satan—the darkness of hate,
He tries to discourage us, but Jesus keeps building our faith.
Whatever God builds, the devil tries but cannot destroy,
He comes with various tricks that he's trying to employ.

The devil promotes strife, God promotes unity,
He is busy destroying lives, but God is busy creating opportunity.
The benefits of serving the Lord are extremely incredible,
In your life he'll create wonders, he'll do the impossible.

Refrain from listening to the voice of the devil,
He will appear in forms that are irresistible.
But God gives strength for today and hope for tomorrow,
He'll bring joy in your life and feeds you just like the sparrow.

Christ in My Valley

When I'm in the valley of the shadow of death
I lift my eyes to Christ; He has never failed me yet.
When my valley gets dark I know somewhere there is light,
My life is protected by the whole armour of Christ.

When my valley gets cold He keeps me warm,
I know I am safe in His tender, loving arms.
He promises to shelter me from all of life's storms
And securely protects me from all of life's harms.

When my valley gets too rough, the hills I try to climb,
I take things into my own hands thinking God isn't on time,
But His soft gentle hands reminds me that the battle is not mine,
I should leave it to Him, on my behalf He will fight.

When my valley gets too low and I can't get out of it,
I cry out to the Lord for Him to give me a lift.
My valleys keep me humble; they prepare me for my hills,
No matter how steep they are, God will help me climb them still.

When I get tired of climbing I stop to rest a while,
He offers me living water from the well that never runs dry.
My hills prepare me for the mountain tops, tall sunny and bright,
All my dreams and aspirations are now in clear sight.

As I bathe in happiness my past I leave behind,
But I'm still humbled by the hills that I once had to climb.

Amazing Clay

It's amazing how a lump of clay could be molded into a being like me,
So robust and strong, yet so feeble and weak.
This clay, so blessed with perfect mind, senses and heart,
Has allowed sin and its consequences to cause it to fall apart.

Clay, fashioned into perfect being corrupted by the world and its selfish needs,
Yet God has blessed me with his grace, which He has given totally free.
The grace that God has given me is an undeserved favor.
Without this grace I face great danger.

There is nothing on earth with value that can purchase His love,
But through His mercy He protects me, I am His beloved.
He is my creator and sustainer, Rock of ages cleft for me,
He has made Himself available; I can hide myself in thee.

His compassion, forgiveness and abundant mercies,
Has shielded me from discouragement and despair- my most feared enemies.
He has deep understanding of my weaknesses and sufferings,
And He readily pardons me despite my short comings.

God does not punish me as my sins deserve,
He extends His hand towards me, mercies that I haven't earned.
Really I deserve death; eternal judgment in the lake of fire,
But my eternal destruction is not God's desire.

Unseen Hands

Did you see the hands that protected you today?
Those strong but gentle hands, which guarded you throughout the day.
They didn't pull away even when you forgot to pray,
Those forbearing hands of mercy from you they didn't stray.

Did you see the hands that kept the bus on the road?
Or the loose bolts on the wheel that His hand had to hold?
When you missed your step you were supposed to fall,
But His hands came to help you even before you called.

The man you didn't see behind you, had a gun tucked in his waist,
His intention was to kill you but God stopped him in his place.
The night you felt the pain in your chest, you were being called by death,
But God said it wasn't time for you to take your last breath.

Did you see the nail that was hidden in the ground?
Or the stranger in the bushes who hid without a sound?
The devil has set traps for you he wants to see you dead,
But the Lord keeps reaching out His hands protecting you instead.

Hell's Highway

Wide as an ocean, smooth as a sea,
Beautiful as a garden, filled with glamour and glee.
No speed limits, no caution signs,
The highway to hell is cleverly designed.

The directions are misleading; they'll send you where you don't intend to go,
You'll think you have it figured out, until you realize that you don't know.
The ride is relaxing; it'll make you feel quite good,
Hell's highway is quite normal, but it is often misunderstood.

Paved with good intentions, you'll think it means you well,
You'll become very complacent, but only time will tell.

There are no turning points and absolutely no round-a-bouts,
This highway is a one way street without a shadow of a doubt.

Hell's highway leads to a dead end- a point of no return,
It takes you to a furnace where you'll forever burn.
Remember, once you get on this highway, it's hard to find an exit,
So be very careful of hell's highway, it's very hard to resist.

Beware

The devil's biggest trick is to make you believe he doesn't exist.
He makes wrong seems right and makes evil hard to resist.
He disguises himself as an angel of light,
And appears sweet and innocent like a lamb in your sight.

He'll make the wicked prosper, forcing you to believe,
That evil works are worthwhile, he'll have you deceived.
He'll blind your eyes and leave you in a state of darkness,
Making you turn to him whenever you feel hopeless.

He'll make very attractive, the ugliest and darkest sins,
And make you think you are victorious in a race that's impossible to win.
He'll make you view the ills of the world as if they are obsolete,
And trap you in his deadly world which is full of conceit.

The devil is the master mind of all deceptions,
He is the author, creator and designer of illusions.
Shun the very appearance of this sly old beast,
He'll use you as a meal for him and his angels to feast

*History,
Culture
and Beliefs*

Beliefs Kill, Beliefs Cure

They say belief kills and belief cures,
Superstitions have open and closed many doors.
We have seen where myths, taboos and superstitious beliefs
Have either caused pains or offer great relief.

They say don't open an umbrella inside the house,
It will bring bad luck and you won't marry your spouse.
And if you get married and you want the marriage to last,
During the reception don't ever break a glass.

If you are pregnant don't you dare climb a fence,
Your child will become a thief and you will have to run to his defense.
If your son resembles the mother luck shall be by his side,
But if he resembles the father, with him bad luck shall abide.

Red underwear is supposed to be worn,
After your spouse is dead and you start to mourn.
Don't sweep dust outside your house at nights,
All your luck will disappear from your sight.

If your palm itches, money you shall get,
Riches are in store for you so don't you fret.
A man should never climb a papaya tree or impotent he shall be,
And getting children is a dream that he will never see.

Never bite your finger after pointing at a grave,
Or else you won't be able to ever give a finger wave.
Belief really kills and belief really cures,
Hold on to your beliefs if your heart they reassure.

On the Other Side

It's a common perception that the grass is greener on the other side,
So I'm thinking that the grass must be more fertile on the other side.
This misconception has caused many to cross to the other side,
Leaving everything behind just to see what's on the other side.
When they realize what is really on the other side,
They curse the very day when they left for the other side.

Here is the grim reality of what goes on over on the other side,
Then when I'm done, you decide if you want to cross over to the other side.
The weather is bi-polar over on the other side,
It's dark, cold and scary over on the other side.
Some people work 3 jobs to survive over on the other side,
Because nothing is for free over on the other side.

Every man for himself, over on the other side,
They'll tear you down to build themselves over on the other side.
Depression is a way of life, over on the other side,
And racism is a reality over on the other side.
Education is needed to unlock opportunities on the other side,
Or else you'll be enslaved over on the other side.

Many are suffering over on the other side,
But pride keeps them from crossing back to the other side.
So before you disrupt your life and leave for the other side,
Take care of the grass over on your side,
You might just have to cross over back to that side.
Remember, the grass is not always greener over on the other side.

Destination Canada

Canada is cold, that's a fact that we all know,
It's known for its maple leaf tree and it's pure, white snow.
It's very multi-cultural and its economy is very great,
The summer sun rises early and sets very late.

An attractive destination, that was what I thought,
I'm leaving Jamaica and I'm going up north.
So I packed my bags and bid my folks goodbye,
We didn't hold back the tears, we didn't even try.

Destination Winnipeg, here I come,
I was a tropical boy all the way from Jamdung.
Leaving the land of my birth for the country of my dreams,
It was an accomplishment that made me feel very supreme.

My long lived dream soon became a nightmare,
The reality of the north had me trembling with fear.
I jumped from an oven and landed in an ice box,
It was like running from a wolf and landing on a fox.

I looked all around me and everything was white,
At first it was amazing, it was an incredible sight.
But then my ears got numb, I couldn't feel my toes,
My fingers got swollen and I lost the use of my nose.

I was told not to cry in winter; I thought it was a silly advice,
But I realized it was a fact because my tears actually turned to ice.
I tried not to breathe too hard; I was blinded by my exhale,
My teeth shattered as I trembled, and my eyes and face got pale.

Six layers of clothing was certainly not enough,
I looked like a black Santa wearing clothing that made me puff.
I actually feared the outdoors; it was more than I could take,
So I humbly hibernated indoors for my own soul's sake.

But winter can be beautiful if you are the adventurous type,
From snowboarding to ice skating, and exploring lots of beautiful sites.
But snow covered mountain tops and frozen, solid lakes,
Was too much for an island boy, it was more than I could take.

So I packed my bags and I waved goodbye,
The fear of freezing on this iceberg was a reasonable alibi.
I'm not accustomed to ice lakes; I'm used to blue sea and white sand,
I have no business in a country whose climate I cannot withstand.

A Glimpse in the Past

Flying bleach bottle planes, pushing coaster and wheel,
Riding boarded scooter bikes or playing sword and shield,
Making paper planes, paper boats and paper guns too,
These are a part of my childhood, how about you?

The only electronic game we knew back then was called the Genesis,
And only a few wealthy persons had it on their premises.
The graphics on the TV set showed only black and white,
And the programmes on television signed off before midnight.

Analog ruled; there were no digital TV remote,
Our favourite Sunday matinee was called the Love Boat.
Pink Panther, Popeye and Thunder Cat kept us entertained,
Life was all about simplicity, that's how we kept sane.

Schools were a safe haven; criminal elements wouldn't touch us there,
Teachers were respected by all; they were revered.
Climbing trees and running wild gave us much exercise,
Back then we didn't depend on social media to actually socialize.

We knew the value of work; we had various chores to do,
Whether balancing a bucket of water on our heads or polishing
  father's shoe.
Each child was raised by the village; we had many moms and dads,
To disrespect an elder, we had to be quite mad.

Those were the days; golden days of the past,
Those memories are little blessings that I wish could last.
Simplicity of life gave us much peace of mind,
Oh how unfortunate we are that days like those are lost behind.

Fun Cyaan Done

Girls running for shelter covering their heads,
Screaming like maniacs as if trying to raise the dead,
Making crazy noises and finding cover under beds,
They are afraid of the roaring thunder so very loud and dread.

For us boys it was the opposite, it was time for fun,
From the angry rains not a boy would run,
Hours of rain ball would have just begun,
Continuous playing even after the rain is done.

Girls holding down there dresses walking without ease,
Not hiding their disgust at the angry breeze,
Curious boys looking but the girls are quite displeased,
Looking at them with distaste as if they are a disease.

But this is the moment when the kites come flying high,
Boys finding the hilltops creating magic in the sky,
Colourful man made birds, dancing pleasingly to the eye,
Like ships on the sea, so through the air they fly.

Girls pulling out umbrellas hiding from the sun,
Boys take advantage of the heat as through the bushes they run,
Whether it be summer, spring, winter, or autumn,
Boys make the best of every season, 'fun cyaan done.'

Colours of Jamaica

Jamaica means "one Love" to the free spirited man,
A place described as a culturally diverse nation.
We appreciate our skank, reggae and dancehall songs,
Weh mek we party all night inna dancehall session.

Jamaica means **black**; it goes beyond the color of our skin,
It shows the true depth of our pain and sufferings.
It shows our dedication, talents and our many skills.

Black means beauty, it also means we are strong willed.
Black goes to show our true ambitions.
Black has fought slavery, conquered colonial oppression,
Black has taken up some of the world's greatest positions.
We continue to show the world the strength of the black nation.

Jamaica means *green*, progress is a must,
We are moving forward, we are ambitious.
Setting the stage for excellence, our determination says it all,
Leaving a mark wherever we go, whether near or far.
We are young fresh and green, proud of our growth,
Despite trials and hardships, we are taking control.
Whether through our songs or with our athletes,
Jamaica, we are proud to be green.

Jamaica means *gold*, golden indeed,
We shine bright like the sun, always creating heat.
Our talents show it all, we are among the elite,
Our tenacity make us hard to defeat.
Our radiant smiles and "No Problem" attitude,
Warm heartedness and spirit of gratitude,
Our Proud appearance and humble nature,
Will help us take control of the future.

Jamaica means Black, Green and Gold
Strong, free and bold.

Image of Dancehall

A colourful art form surrounded by many controversy,
Dancehall; a lifestyle …a culture … a tradition full of hypocrisy.
It claims to expose ugly truths and acts as a voice for the poor,
Claiming that the source of injustice must be uprooted; no longer to
   be obscure.

It is a fact that this colorful culture is all some persons know,
This is how their parents grew, and this is how their children will grow.

But it's sad that this "no problem culture" has failed to accept its social responsibilities,
It doesn't even try to conceal the nature of its many hostilities.

It is sad that this culture indigenous to the Jamaican face,
Is now turning out to be our most failing grace.
Dancehall, by many, is placed on a high pedestal,
And oftentimes overlooked is the fact that it lacks values, both moral and ethical.

Dancehall, slowly being transformed into a culture of lawlessness,
Where guns, money, killing and drugs are abused without a sense of cautiousness.
Prominent faces of dancehall try to walk above the law,
But feeling untouchable and invincible is normally their tragic flaw.

Vastly becoming a societal destructive factor,
The distaste of modern dancehall is eating away our moral ethics like cancer.
A monster creating a generation of monsters, driving fear across the land,
It has become a force that we can no longer tolerate or withstand.

We'll never be contented with the demonic images used,
Or the derogatory messages in lyrical content or other messages of abuse.
It's not our intention to fight dancehall; it is one of Jamaica's economic tools,
We simply want to clean it up so it can be less crude.

Gentleman

I reached out to hold her hands as she descended the stairs,
But the reaction that she gave me, made me pull back in fear.
She rolled her eyes and snapped at me, immediately I grew scared,
And then she said, "You pertinent boy, touch me if you dare."

I pulled out her chair for her to sit; she didn't even say thanks,
But instead she turned away and asked, "What's wrong with this
    young man?"
I didn't get offended because of the persistent gentleman I am,
So I smiled at her and politely asked, "May I take your jacket ma'am"?

She got upset, stomped her feet and said, "Look here man,
Likkle bwoy stop perplex me, do I look like I have deformed hands?
Mi can do things fi mi self, yes likkle bwoy I can,
Don't you see that I am a strong, independent Jamaican?"

As astonished as I was, I said, "Ma'am, I understand,
But please don't get it twisted; I also am a Jamaican man.
Mi grow up a Garlands bush bush, mi nyam plenty okra and yam,
Mi tie out hog, cow, donkey and goat, and mi bade out a bath pan."

But that still nuh hinda mi, like you, yes I can,
Come a foreign, hold on pan mi roots and represent fi all Jamaican man.
I pride myself to show the world that Jamaica can produce a real gentleman.

Jamaica Will

The vision is ours I see it clear,
When Jamaica shall awake from this terrible nightmare.
Men cannot walk the streets without fear,
And there is no concern for child or elderly care.

A new Jamaica must be seen,
The same Jamaica in our forefather's dreams.
A Jamaica where love fills the once bloody streets,
And the guns are replaced with love and harmony.

A Jamaica where the economy becomes stabilized,
And education, health and welfare become prioritized.
We all need to fight for what Garvey visualized,
Until his dreams for Jamaica becomes actualized.

We are hardworking people, we don't need pity,
What we need is fairness, justice and equality.
We need them to open doors and provide opportunity,
So we can build and maintain a better society.

The vision is ours, it is very near,
The voices of the poor everyone will hear.
We will enjoy Jamaica, the land we love so dear,
And create a future filled with prosperity, love and care.

Foreigner

She left with black hair, came back blonde,
Leaving home the right way, came back wrong.
She left dark skinned, came back looking half white,
The weird colour combination was not a pretty sight.

Her new appearance was not appealing,
The entire town found her amusing.
This brown eye girl came back with blue eyes
We didn't know if it was real or it was a disguise.

Her lips were fat; she looked like a fox,
She proudly introduced us to what was Botox.
The piercing in her nose matched the one above her eye,
She was taking fashion to a new high.

Her gold chain must have weighed 20 pounds,
And her arms full of bangles made musical sounds.
Her nails were long until they were bent,
She really thought she was heaven sent.

Her eyelashes were long and curved upwards too,
Only reason you could see her eyes was because of the bright blue.
The tattoo on her shoulder read "sexy till death,"
But sexy has left her and she hasn't taken her last breath.

History, Culture and Beliefs

This woman thinks she's the definition of beauty,
But what she has done is self-inflicted cruelty.
The way she spoke made us all laugh,
The patois mixed with "twanglish" was like her personal craft.

Foreign can give, Foreign can take,
Foreign can build, Foreign can break.
Place your mind in a positive state,
Because many clowns foreign has been known to make.

Black Inventors

Throughout history blacks have made significant contributions,
They have helped to improve the living condition of all nations.
Their remarkable inventions have enhanced the lives of man,
To them we need to give standing ovation.

Garret Morgan, son of a former slave, invented the gas mask.
In the midst of racial oppression, he took up a worthwhile task.
He also had a great idea to control traffic flow,
A device that would advise you whether to stop or to go.

The T-shaped traffic light he invented,
On November 20, 1923, in his name it was patented.
In 1912 he made smoke protectors for fire fighters too,
Seems like there was nothing this Garret Morgan couldn't do.

We give credit to Thomas Edison for the light bulb invention,
But Lewis Latiman made it practical to be used in everyday life situation.
He introduced carbon filament light bulb; it was economical, efficient and safe,
Without its invention this world would be a much darker place.

Elijah McCoy a brilliant black inventor,
Revolutionized the world with his steam engine lubricator.
So if you are of high quality, don't get offended or become annoyed,
When someone describes you as the real McCoy.

Dr. Charles Richard Drew, to you we express thanks,
For impressively inventing the revolutionary blood bank.
Your innovative invention has saved countless lives
Because of you many persons have survived.

Perishable items can be transported near or far,
The automatic refrigeration system can be built in a truck or car.
We can now enjoy foods indigenous to different parts of the globe,
We salute you Frederick M. Jones, your story will forever be told.

We pay homage to black inventors; we pause to recognize your work,
Your brilliant minds and skilful hands have helped to change the world.
During times of oppressions and moments of calamity,
You worked hard in different ways to change the course of black history.

Nelson Mandela

From prisoner to president he went,
Some say he was a legend, others say he was heaven sent.
Humility defined his life, he sacrificed his freedom for what was right,
And to a dark nation he became their light.
A man of valor who clearly had no fear,
Was unfairly sent to prison for twenty seven years,
For many this would be the end of their story,
But this man rose from captivity and brought South Africa glory.
His embodiment of stoicism, forbearance and pardon,
Has helped him to rise from extra- ordinary to stardom.
He was a recipient of the Nobel Peace Prize,
He was destined for greatness, his limit was the skies.
This giant for justice has left a great legacy behind,
He was the epitome of greatness and courage combined.
He was proven to be a great moral and political leader,
His life wasn't just a lesson; it has being a great teacher.
He has sewn seeds of virtue; his toiling was long and hard,
But he reaped a fruitful harvest, great was his reward.
He is the symbol of the fight for human rights and social equality,
Who became the first president of South Africa to be elected democratically.

He was devoted to education, democracy and equality,
And he led his country with much integrity and dignity.
His life has been an inspiration to all who face oppression,
We can rise from a fall and make great progression.
A man full of charisma has sadly passed on,
A nation has lost one of its greatest sons.
Nelson Mandella will never be forgotten,
In the hall of fame his name will be written.
In the streets his name will be shouted with pride,
From prisoner to president, his legacy will survive.

Luther's Dream

August 28, 1963, Martin Luther King Jr. spoke of a dream,
A dream in which the black nation of America was free.

Martin Luther King Jr. had a clear vision.
He and other civil leaders led a group of many thousands,
They marched down the busy streets of U.S.A's Capital, Washington,
Where they protested against the manacles of segregation.

They wanted to break free the chains of discrimination.
This march was a brave decision, knowing that they risked
   facing persecution.
These heroes were driven by great determination.
They urgently needed a change in their inhumane conditions.

These men were tired of the unspeakable horrors of police brutality.
They were fed up of extreme poverty in a country with growing prosperity.
Citizens of colour simply wanted to be treated equally,
It was full time that the black nation enjoyed a taste of democracy.

He charged the people to protest in peace, but to march without fear.
He envisioned that one day racial injustice would cease; change was near.
He told them not to wallow in the valley of despair,
But to the true cause they should remain sincere.

He told them not to drink from the cup of bitterness; the dark days
   shall past,
The harsh reality that they were experiencing would not last.
Even though the scope of their sufferings were indeed vast
They would one day be able to say, "Thank God, we are free at last."

Racial Barriers

I'm giving truth to a lie that I now know exist,
That racial equality and freedom is all a myth.
We are tricked into believing that there is equal opportunity for all,
Truth be told, that is an illusion that makes the oppressed appalled.

We need to acknowledge the reality of the world that we are living in,
Where color of skin matters, and quality of character is dim.
Riches and fame will get you wherever you need to go,
And friends in high places are important; it's all about who you know.

Positions are given to persons with recognized surnames,
Whether qualified or not, it's about popularity and fame.
Skin color and hair texture and pre-requisites to work in some institutions,
So yes, we are still held down by discrimination.

So because of fear of inferiority, some folks lighten their skin with bleach,
Hoping this will give them acceptance and allow them higher places
   to reach.
If they could peel off their skin like Joseph's coat they would,
Because society has taught them that the less color, the more good.

But I stand boldly to say to you with pride,
Under subjections to inequality we have made many great strides.
Top sportsmen to great architects, great doctors, and presidents too,
We continue to break racial barriers, and that's what we'll continue to do.

Mental Slavery

Physically free from shackles and chains,
No more buck master beating us insane.
Free from the cracking of whips on our backs,
We have to fight hard never to go back.

Working all day whether rain or shine,
We couldn't read a watch so we couldn't tell time.
We couldn't plan to go home to eat a perfect meal,
The cruel judgment of man gave us a raw deal.

They broke our hearts but our spirit remained strong,
We knew how to live amidst destitution.
We told lots of stories, sang lots of songs,
While the brave among us planned their revolution.

Emancipation is a must, independence must be,
We break away the chains of captivity.
Thanks to God we are physically free,
We must now emancipate ourselves from mental slavery.

Oppression

Oppression is the key to the wicked's prosperity,
It's a means for their wealth to come to fertility.
They maintain power and control when we are trapped in poverty.
They skilfully keep us entrapped in a new form of slavery.

They test us to see our level of bravery,
And arm us with weapons to destroy fellow humanity,
Therefore promoting the increase level of brutality,
Which builds a wall of hopelessness in our society.

They increase the cost of living and decrease job opportunity.
Education is a luxury enjoyed mostly by the wealthy.

They force us to think that we can only survive by doing things illegally,
Which further diminishes the need for our dependency on spirituality.

We can overcome by decreasing illiteracy and improving numeracy,
And work together to achieve full democracy.
Let's pressure the system to give more accountability,
And charge the leaders to pay attention to their responsibility.

Self-Inferiority

Trapped in ignorance, enslaved by our minds,
Our eyes are fully open, yet still we are blind.
We abuse all kinds of chemical, destruction to mankind,
Just to get a clearer skin colour or to feel refined.

Our hearts shamefully lusts after another man's complexion,
Ashamed to look in the mirror at our own reflection.
The colour of our skin doesn't change the quality of our character,
We can change the course of our lives, colour doesn't matter.

We ink our bodies seeking some form of recognition,
Not realizing we are marching down a path of destruction.
It is time we wake up to the realization,
That these senseless acts only add to the degradation of the black nation.

How can we be angry when others think of themselves as superior?
When we behave in ways that indicate that we are inferior.
We are the ones giving them that great power,
Let's embrace our ethnicity, and believe in what we stand for.

Malcolm X stood when it was difficult to stand,
Martin Luther King and King Jr. stood, they weren't afraid to stand,
Marcus Garvey stood; these men were willing to stand,
Let us all be brave and say, "I stand."

My "N" Word

I choose to use the 'N' word however I please,
When I spread my lips the word comes out with ease.
Don't you dare judge me; I don't need to be chastised,
My carefully chosen 'N' word will catch you by surprise.

I can use my 'N' word anywhere I so desire,
I don't have to whisper, no special setting is required.
I won't be criticized or be the centre of any heated debate,
To my little 'N' word, many persons can relate.

My 'N' word is a noun, it's a city located in Southeastern France,
Many did not know this fact when at the word they first took a glance.
This is also a descriptive word which is used quite a lot,
It is also one of your most favorite words whether you realize it or not.

Sometimes it's used hypocritically, giving compliments by default,
But one can never say it is used to give any kind of assault.
Even though provocative, it often bring lots of smiles,
I don't know what your 'N' word is, but my 'N' word is NICE.

Adrenaline Rush

Flying down the track at the speed of light,
Making circles round and round like an insane cock fight.
Sitting on four wheels, protected by a helmet on your head,
Making a bomb on four wheels as comfortable as your bed.

There must be some great adrenaline rush from wrestling with a bull,
Violently twisting and turning, pushing and pull.
No line of defense between you and that terrible beast,
Staring death in its face; for you there is no defeat.

Knocking fist to fist, in a competitive, brutish fight,
Suffering bruised and battered face and long term blurry sight.

To give that last blow one is willing to pay any price,
Even if that means facing a hard demise.

Climbing tall towers or crossing Niagara Falls on a rope,
And with the pressures of facing death one is still able to cope,
Jumping from a plane; dancing in the air,
Doing what they do without any form of terror or fear.

Living precious life on the edge, just to entertain,
Cheating death in ways that proves to be brutally insane.
How can we describe it- is it crude, cold or bold?
Gambling with a gift that cannot be bought or sold.

Wealth

Being rich is not about how much you have, but about how much you give,
It's not about where you reside, but the quality of life you live.
It's about having warmth, love and happiness stored in your heart,
And the ability to spread joy to those whose lives are torn apart.

Being rich is about using the little that you have to do big things in people's lives,
Knowing that your generous giving is helping to make others thrive.
A kind heart and a giving hand will bring gratification to every soul,
And make a fire of jubilance burn within you without control.

If one should measure richness by wealth and poverty by the lack of it,
Or success by material and educational acquisition and failure by been a misfit,
Happiness by your broad laughter and sadness by the flowing tears,
This world would be an even sicker place, filled with more pain, more sorrows and more fears.

But for those who are not blinded and clearly are able to see,
That richness, success and happiness doesn't just come by materialistically,
Are the ones who will experience true happiness and true joy.
Therefore true wealth, richness and success they will be able to enjoy.

Exposed

They hate what they can't fix,
Destroy what they can't understand,
They fear what they can't conquer,
Give you more than you can withstand.

They want to eliminate you,
But your will is just too strong,
They hide the right from you,
Just to trap you in doing the wrong.

They envy your resilience,
Find ways to make you weak,
They pretend they want to build you,
But your destruction is what they seek.

They help you climb the ladder,
With the hope that you will fall,
They pretend to give a listening ear,
But totally ignore your desperate call.

They are everywhere around you,
You don't have to search long or hard,
Iniquity is found in the prentuous man,
For you they show no kind regard.

Judas

Beware of the Judases among you,
Your enemies are plenty; your friends are quite few.
A kiss from an enemy who you thought was your friend,
Could destroy many bonds that are impossible to mend.

Beware of the Judases who offer you peace of mind,
They will kiss you on the cheek while stabbing you from behind.

They will seek to deceive you, destroying your life.
Your closest friend can be your Judas; Samson's Judas was his wife.

Be careful of the kisses of deception,
Especially from the persons in whom you see perfection,
With just one kiss you can be deceived.
And the Judas in them is eventually revealed.

Be careful that a Judas is not hidden in you,
Because your enemies will be plenty and your friends will be few.
A kiss from you who they thought they knew,
Could change their life in a way or two.

Love

Four letters containing powers beyond measure,
Often misused to gain all sorts of selfish pleasure.
Four letters that are treated like a polysemous word,
Taking a word with greatness, making it so absurd.

One word, found on the tip of every one's tongue,
Used recklessly and dangerously by the old and the young.
This little word has lost its meaning; it has clearly lost its purpose,
Painfully used as a mockery and in many lives have caused havoc.

Actions show fondness, but it is described by using love,
It is echoed like a broken record, it is even bellowed to the Supreme above.
A great father once said "I love you", for the world he sent his son to die,
And now carnal man says the same thing, by making their fellow men cry.

The world has subconsciously substituted the feeling of the weaker for the stronger,
Causing many to fear the little word, believing the true meaning exists no longer.
This word is misinterpreted, even though it's used a lot,
But once you start abusing the word it's quite difficult for you to stop.

So next time you chose to use the word 'LOVE,' make sure it's from the heart,
Let your actions prove as much, otherwise please don't start.
Remember the misuse of this word can cause a lot of pain,
So please don't make it a practice to use this word in vain.

Hate

Another four letters ... why do we love to hate?
Hypocrites we are, so much hate we create.
We preach out against inhumane treatment and everything else,
We say we grow to love, but in our heart hate dwells.

To hate, many have become pre-disposed,
Many say they love, until they have become exposed.
They show a loving face, but hate eats away their flesh,
Hate becomes a part of them ... Haters until death.

Every day we wake, LOVE we say,
We fall prostrate at His feet, to the God of love we pray.
We teach our kids the right; but still we do the wrong,
And when we are in the light, we demonstrate love that's really strong.

But when eyes are shut, and we go behind the scenes,
When night pushes its curtains down, and we are hidden by darkness' screen,
The monster hidden in us raises its ugly head,
And instead of spreading love, we vent hate instead.

What's sad is that when it's convenient we think hate can be justified,
As long as our selfish ego is thoughtlessly satisfied.
But this monster that we create will eat us alive,
So we better turn from hate to love, that's the key to a happy life.

My Brother's Keeper

I am nothing if I am not my brother's keeper,
A man who sows love will be a happy reaper.
The choices we make shows the true nature of our character,
We can choose to be selfish or selfless, helping one another.

The kindness we show to the least of men,
Is a symbol of the kindness you show to the God of Israel.
Whosoever is kind to the poor lends to the Lord,
For the kind deeds they have done, great will be their reward.

We live in a very individualistic culture,
A culture that encourages us to be selfish to each other.
We selfishly hoard the spoils of our labour,
Totally forgetting to share with the poor who suffers.

It is in our nature to be selfish and proud,
Blowing our own trumpets, making our own sounds.
Pride gives us the illusion that we are floating on clouds,
We need humility to bring us down to level ground.

What am I if I cannot share my brother's pain?
I would be living a lie that will all be in vain.
It's not too late to lend a hand to one who's down
Without making a murmur or showing a frown.

Remember that good you do comes back at you,
When you have bad days it will see you through.
Be your brother's keeper, to you the same he'll do.
Show him genuine kindness, unselfish love that's true.

Rare Friends

It's rare that you find good people; good people with kind heart,
You have showed me the true meaning of kindness right from the
   very start.

The kindness that you hold in your heart, your deeds certainly do show,
Your presence is all that's needed to make a dark room glow.

It's rare that you find a person that smiles for no reason at all,
Your warm spirit and radiance makes the biggest problem seems small.

You are a true heroine because you impact lives in many ways,
For all the good deeds that you have done, long shall be your days.

It's easy to tell the incredible person that you are,
Your jubilance and inner beauty shines like the brightest star.

Continue to make your light shine and your warmth radiate,
You are an incredible person who I am proud to emulate.

.... For Betty ....

Eulogy for the Late Self

Death has proven to be many things to many people.
Certainly it has brought tears, sorrow, heartaches and almost unbearable distress.
There is the exception to this rule where death has brought relief from pain, bondage and relief from stress.
In which category does death to self falls?

I can just imagine that it was a beautiful morning on God's creation – Earth, when Eve, just like anyone of us would foolishly yield to the temptation of the serpent, the devil himself ...
Self was born ...
He is approximately six thousand years old.

Self grew with the determination to cause widespread havoc on the once perfectly created earth.
Self caused mankind to be selfish, unkind, unfriendly, malicious and proud.

It was self that made Cain kill Abel, Potiphar's wife to lie on Joseph, David to commit adultery and murder, Samson to lose his sight and strength, and Judas to betray Jesus.

Many persons have tried to overcome self. Ruth tried when she refused to leave Naomi, the poor widow tried when she fed the profit, the fishermen tried when they left their boats and followed Jesus, but self grew like a parasitic vine as it continued to portray its negative traits.
Self should have died a very painful death when we the Christians were reborned ... but alas! The stubborn character kept on growing.

Today we have decided to allow self to die. Its life ended when the saints of God took the sword, "The Holy Bible," cut self down with the Holy Scriptures and decided to stand on Gods promises.
Today we refuse mourn lukewarmness, lying, stealing, pride ... But rather we celebrate the death of self.
In this instance may death retain its sting forever and ever.

The Bully Coin

At some point in life, to someone, we are an oppressor,
Someone will be intimidated by us; to someone we will be an aggressor.
Likewise it is inevitable that by someone we will be oppressed,
Someone will intimidate us, we will be aggressed.

It happens without us even knowing, we naturally show our might,
We push the weaker down while fighting to stand upright.
We become addicted to the thoughts of reaching to the top,
That we ignore the person whose progress we have thoughtlessly stopped.

Fear will be created whether intentionally or not,
But many resort to using fear as a tool; the only weapon they've got.
Using bullying as a form of expression is indeed low and inconceivable
Using it as an oppressive tool is even more unbelievable.

We will experience life on both sides of the bully coin,
You can conform to societal norms or the hoodlums you can join.

But life as a bully can never be worthwhile,
To no man, woman, animal or child should you ever be hostile.

There are more joys in helping than there are in hurting,
More pleasures from smiling than there are in frowning.
Happiness in life comes from the good seeds you sow,
Fight against bullying …. let the whole world know.

*Dreams,
Hopes &
Aspirations*

Dreams and Aspirations

A man with a dream needs a woman with a vision,
A woman who is confident enough to help him make decisions.
One who can open up her mind to supporting his ambitions,
Helping him to leave a mark for future generations.

A man with a dream needs a woman with dedication-
A woman who will stick by him through any situation.
One who won't criticize his failures but help him find motivation,
She'll help him through difficult times while showing much affection.

A man with a dream needs a woman with aspiration-
A woman who can step away from culture and old traditions.
One who sees personal growth as a meaning transition,
She will be strong enough to show much assertion.

A woman with a vision needs a man with a solutions,
A man who will battle currents and waves to rescue her from persecution.
One who can look in her eyes with nothing but admiration
He'll help her to be all that she can be, putting her in a better position.

A woman with a vision needs a man with direction,
She needs a man who shows forms of high projections.
One who is humble enough to give and accept corrections,
A man who will do everything to help her reach perfection.

A man with a dream needs a woman with a vision.
They will work hand in hand to make great societal contributions,
Together they will help with the development of the nation.
A man with a dream and a woman with a vision will always be a great combination.

We Are the World

I'll help you move the obstacles that you stumble on,
If there are roadblocks that you are afraid to pass, I'll gladly tarry along.
For the river that is too wide to cross, I'll help you build a bridge,
I'll help you walk through the valley or glide over the mountain ridge.

We are the world, each and every single man,
We must fight each other's battles as much and as long as we can.
Your pain becomes my hurt, my fears become yours,
My joys make you smile, happiness shows in galore.

We expect the world to change, but we want to remain the same,
So the world remaining constant, isn't mankind to be blamed?
The change that we seek lies on our own head,
We can choose to lead courageously, or we can choose to be led.

I am the world and that thinking is quite clear,
I must be the change I seek and that reasoning is also fair.
If I change and you change then a new genesis we will see,
A revolution, an unfathomable freedom, a world of love that's a guarantee.

But it all begins with humility and the crucifixion of the 'I' in me,
And to resurrect love globally is something that we can all agree.
Each person can be our brother; each person should be our friend,
In this revolutionized world, on each other we can depend.

Think Big

Opportunities are endless there's much to achieve,
If you work hard and believe, there's much to receive.
Expand your horizons; make your limit be the sky,
But in order to succeed you must first try.

You can only achieve as much as your dreams,
Always aim high no matter how hard it seems.

Dreams, Hopes & Aspirations

Try to get a grasp on life's endless possibilities,
You'll surprise yourself at your different capabilities.

Think big, aim high, determination is the key,
Set attainable goals, be all that you can be.
Set high standards, never settle for lest,
Whatever you do, strive to be your best.

Difficulties are inevitable, but never say you can't,
All things are possible; you can reach it if you want.
Don't just reflect light, instead shine bright like the sun,
Challenge yourself never to be outdone.

Never limit yourself to the things you can do,
If you see it, and you want it, after it you must pursue.
Welcome every obstacle; they'll only make you stronger,
And after every failure you need to try harder.

Along with big dreams comes perseverance,
Don't just think big, find as much endurance.
Work hard at your dreams with much determination,
The land of success will be your final destination.

Gift of Love

When the windows of heaven are open and blessings fall on you,
It may pour like heavy raindrops or just a light dew.
Whether its heavy or light, heaven already knows,
The beauty of the blessings, waiting to be bestowed.

Inside you there's a baby boy a precious gift of love from God,
He knew too well of your needs, so inside you he planted a seed.
God is admonishing you to nurture him well,
So in his little heart His spirit may dwell.

The time God has sent him is just right,
You both are precious in His sight.

This star He has blessed you with will shine bright,
You are the candle stick, he will be the light.

He is a heritage from the Lord,
The fruit of your womb, such a great reward.
He'll fuel your happiness; he's your bundle of joy,
I pray God's richest blessings on you and your baby boy.

Every good and perfect gift comes from above,
This amazing gift is a sign of his perfect love.
Go forth and be a great mom, even though it already shows.
May you and your little bundle of joy grow and glow.

I Can

I dare you to tell me that I can't because I can,
Certain words and attitudes aren't included in my plan.
I will not settle for sitting when I know I can stand,
I hold the keys to my success in the palm of my hands.

Only my best is ever good enough, a motto that I truly believe,
If I should settle for less, then mediocrity is what I'll receive.
I'll push myself to the limit, unleashing the potentials locked in me,
There are too many opportunities, for me to be less than I can be.

If I can't run or walk up the ladder of success, then on my knees will
   I creep,
I'll climb all the hills before me, whether they are low or steep.
I can, I can, I definitely can, and I most certainly will,
I'll strive for excellence always; my best can always be better still.

No matter where life takes you, just remember this one thing,
'CAN'T' is just a word that only failure it will bring.
So whenever you stumble upon roadblocks in life, don't you dare utter
   that word,
'I can' and 'I will' are the only words that must be heard.

Hidden In You

If you can see the lumber that is hidden in a tree,
Or smell the sweet savouring honey waiting to come out of a bee,
If you can taste the sugar that is embedded in the cane,
You can definitely see the rainbow that will come after the rain.

Everything has a purpose and has a story to tell,
Even if it appears to be just an empty shell,
There's potential hidden inside it more than you will ever know,
Even if by looking at it, it really doesn't show.

You cannot measure importance based on a human scale,
A ship is important to a sailor, but to the carpenter so is a nail,
You may think you are an underachiever; you may not see your worth,
But to someone, somewhere, you are the most important thing on
  this earth.

The beauty about an empty glass is that it has the potential to be filled,
Optimism is the key to becoming strong willed,
What you have to offer only you can give,
The life God has planned for you, only you can live.

So if you feel unsuccessful and far from your goals,
Remember, you determine your success, it's your life; you are in control.
Your best is good enough for me if it's good enough for you,
Stay focused on your life and to your own self be true.

Still I Rise

From the slump of the gutter to higher heights—I rise,
Defeating every obstacle, being an element of surprise,
Whether it's destiny or luck, I must survive,
From the slump of the gutter to higher heights—I rise.

Staying down isn't an option, I must not be defeated,
Many prayers I have prayed, many psalms I have repeated,

Certain habits I have dropped, some friends I have deleted,
Many thoughts I have erased, in God I have depended.

So many greats have gone before me; they walked this very road I trod,
They started from nowhere, elevating themselves despite all the odds.
They did it in a time when they were oppressed with chains, whips and rods,
So I know that I can do it with the help of the Almighty God.

Determination is my weapon, education is my key,
Motivation and dedication will help me to be all that I can be.
If you find yourself in a gutter where oppression blinds you so you can't see,
Remember every gutter has an opening, you just have to believe.

New Beginnings

As a new day unfolds, a new page is turned,
The old things are passed away, never to be returned.
Today is yesterday's future, it will be tomorrow's past,
Correct the wrongs of yesterday, today they will not last.

Yesterday's mistakes should be left where they belong,
Leave them behind, don't struggle with them along.
You can't undo what has already being done,
Those burdens will only keep you down.

Cease every opportunity that comes your way,
Remember no one is promised to see a next day.
The present is a gift, unwrap it with care,
Success is within your reach, it is very near.

Focus on the now, the new page you are writing on,
Ensure no mistakes are made; your task should be well done.
And if you have erred there's still time to do it right,
But only your best is good enough if you want to reach great heights.

Mistakes

Never feel threatened by your mistakes,
They'll prepare you for the tests in life that you will have to retake.
Mistakes shine a light on the path that you must trod,
You are like a sheep; your mistake is like a rod.

Your mistakes in life will be your greatest teacher,
They will teach you lessons that will help you go further.
Misguided judgment doesn't have to lead to a path of failure,
But they certainly have a lot to do with determining your future.

You can repeat the same error which means you haven't learnt,
Or you can use it as an example, to which you never will return.
Disappointments and mistakes are tools that will help you find the right way,
As long as you leave them behind where they were meant to stay.

A mistake is really a great learning experience,
It can lead to brilliance which also boosts self-confidence.
Remember that the strongest gets weak, the wisest makes error,
But the most successful person learns most from his failures.

Mistakes can make you weak; mistakes can make you strong,
Build on the things you do right, correct the things you did wrong.
To grow you have to try, sometimes when you try you will fail,
Failure proves that you have tried, so try and try again.

Dreams

Dreams don't come through overnight,
Sometimes you have to struggle, sometimes you have to fight.
Dreams motivate us to press on a little longer,
They encourage us to fight harder and they make you stronger.

Dreams keeps us working, work keeps us sane,
Only those with a dream have something to gain.

Dreams keep us alive; a man without dreams is dead,
It is better for him to stay curled up in his bed.

Dreams leads to success, success leads to bigger dreams,
Never stop dreaming no matter how impossible it seems.
Great things are built on dreamers' dreams and visionary visions,
Who all knew failure was a possibility but for them it wasn't an option.

They knew attempts could fail, but great lessons failure could teach.
A great lesson teaches wisdom, higher heights must be reached.
Don't give up on your dreams, even if you fail,
Dreams do come through, it is never too late.

Lost

When you are lost and can't find your way,
Your compass has been broken and it's near the end of day,
Your mind starts to wander and your heart begins to fear,
That there's no hope for you as night is drawing near.

You have no one to point you in the direction you should go,
You are clueless as to where you are … you simply just don't know.
You would give anything in exchange for a ray of hope,
To carry you through your crisis, no sympathy to be evoked.

When troubles like wildfire knocks feverishly at your door,
And sorrows like heavy rainfall suddenly begins to pour,
Your heart becomes weak from all the grief and pain,
There's no greatness to lose, no victory to gain.

But that one glimpse of hope is all that you need,
The ray of light behind the cloud will push you far indeed.
A drowning man will do anything to keep himself afloat,
He'll climb on a single straw just to reach his boat.

So if you are lost and can't find your way, don't worry, you can be found.
Great days are ahead, you are homeward bound.

A broken compass can send you exactly where you need to be,
Sometimes you have to get lost to open your eyes and see.

You Are

If you are working real hard trying to put food on the table,
Don't complain; be grateful that you're able.
You're capable of doing things that others only dream about,
Thank God for not allowing the devil to put you on time out.

Be proud of the progress that you're comfortably making,
It's time to eliminate all the friends that you know are faking.
As life gets harder you'll keep getting stronger,
You have no time for mediocrity; you don't need pessimism any longer.

Each day that you get older, you'll keep looking younger,
Continue to amaze yourself; you're like the toy soldier.
For all the pain in your life, you finally brought closure,
So if they want to hurt you, they won't get that pleasure.

Life is all about freedom, freedom enables progression,
You are still in bondage if your life shows regression.
Embrace freedom by moving forward, one step at a time,
Take control of what's yours, respect what is mine.

Count your many blessings each and every single day,
Be grateful for this gift of life and humbly stop to pray.
The bridges that you've struggled to crossed, you should never burn,
There will come a time in life when to them you may have to return.

Be careful how you treat the persons you past on your way up,
Share your blessings with them; remember God has filled your cup.
You might pass those persons on your way down, if you should ever fall,
And on those same persons you might just have to call.

Past and Present

So many mistakes made,
So many lessons learnt,
So many bridges crossed,
So many bridges burnt.

So many mountains climbed,
So many skies soared,
So many windows closed,
So many open doors.

Too many lives lost,
Too many in the grave,
Too many misfortunes,
Too many souls unsaved.

Too many dreams shattered,
Too many hopes destroyed,
Too many faiths weakened,
Too many lost joys.

So from hence on forth,
Plan to make a change,
No more reckless living,
Strive not to be estrange.

Rise

You will often times be defeated,
But your story doesn't have to end,
Defeat doesn't mean that you are broken,
It simply means try again.

A defeat is just a lesson,
That teaches you quite well,
That a defeat that turns into a victory,
Is quite a great story to tell.

So the next time you face a defeat,
And you lose sight of your way,
Just remember that only failure beats a trial,
So 'I Quit' you must not say.

If you quit you plan to lose,
And with that mentality you can never win,
But with a positive mind and a strong will,
Your race to success will begin.

So be persistent, be resilient,
Never you dare stop try,
Remember, behind every success story,
Someone had to cry.

Greater Things

Ignore what they say, love who you are,
If your goal is to succeed you will no doubt reach far.
No one can set your limit; make it reach the sky,
Impossible is just a word that should force you to try.

Choose to be outstanding, let the whole world see,
That one can rise above poverty and be all that you can be.
Being poor is no longer a reason to stay behind the rest,
It is no longer a barrier but should motivate you to do your best.

From nothing to something, that's what some say,
But you were never nothing, throw those thoughts away.
As you transition through different stages, you may accomplish more,
But each stage would have paved the way for each open door.

Having a humble beginning is a luxury in disguise,
It teaches you many lessons on how to creatively improvise.
These lessons will help you along the path to accomplishment,
From something to greater things, many will be left in astonishment.

But it shouldn't be a surprise when humble stars rise,
To ever doubt our capabilities have been proven to be unwise.
With humility and assertiveness we surpass all expectations,
We can become everything that would blow the wildest imaginations.

I am a Multitude

I am a multitude; I am more than one,
The person that you see is more like a combination.
I am a multitude of expression, a multitude of fear,
A multitude of depression, a multitude of tears.

If you see my back been broken, I'm carrying a multitude of cares,
The multitude within me sometimes gives me a scare.
If I sound confusing, don't be too alarmed,
It's the multitude within me, on a quest to be transformed.

Where there are many, there must be controversy,
I am a multitude of greats, a powerful oligarchy.
There's a great dissension going on in my head,
This multitude is angry, doesn't want to be misled.

I seem to be a confused; perceived to be a contradiction,
This multitude of arrogance is causing great friction.
This multitude of regiment serves its own purpose,
It organizes electric thoughts that provoke others to become curious.

So when you see me acting all careless or confused,
It's the multitude inside whose voice of instruction I cannot elude.
This multitude of greatness, this multitude of despair,
One moment I embrace it, next moment I want it to disappear.

I am a multitude of expression; I am more than one,
The person that you see is indeed a combination.
A combination of greatness, a combination of fear,
A combination of weakness, a combination I hold so dear.

Reflection

The reflection in the mirror is an extra-ordinary one,
It is the reflection of a very humble but proud man.
The reflection shows a man who was on a path of destruction,
A man who has now risen above all fear and intimidation.

A man now on a path that shows great progression,
Having no intentions of showing any form of regression.
The reflection in the mirror shows a man who once failed,
A man who almost used his hands to dig his own grave.

It shows a man who has been battered and severely bruised,
A man who wasted many years being angry and confused.
The reflection shows a man who was lost and had nothing to lose,
A man who was just empty and simply bemused.

What is reflected in the mirror is a determined man,
One who has jumped many hurdles that have helped him to stand.
The obstacles he has overcome have made him strong,
He welcomes optimism, to pessimism he says so long.

The old reflection has died, a new image has been born,
An image that's not broken, an image that's not torn.
An image that isn't scorched, an image that no longer mourns,
An image that is pleasant, turning its frown upside down.

When I look at the reflection that's looking back at me,
It appears to be as happy as one can ever be.
It knows it has triumphed, it knows it has overcome,
To you reflection I say job well done.

When you look in the mirror what do you see?
Do you see a reflection that has been all that it can be?
Do you see a reflection that smiles at you?
Does it feel good that it has done all that it can do?

Game Over

Living your dreams, killing my vision,
I wasn't thinking clear when I made that decision.
I care about your life; you don't care about mine,
You are all about you, all of the time.

Your dreams are so big; they make me look small,
I'm scared to look up because your ego is so tall.
Your love is conditional, it doesn't stretch far,
Your heart is locked up for life behind your own bars.

Release me from your cage so I can spread my wings and fly,
Even if my dreams fade away, I know I would have tried.
These eyes are focused far and wide; I am going to soar,
Release me so I can find the will to open my own doors.

I'm tired of holding you up so you won't have to fall,
You already own the court, now you want to take the ball.
But if you try to hold me down, you have to stay down with me,
I'm breaking all the chains; I'm setting myself free.

I'm locking the door behind me; I'm shutting it forever,
I'm bidding you goodbye, forever and ever.
It's obvious that you and I will never make it together,
So pack your ego, this game is over.

Just Until

It won't last forever, it is just until,
There will come a time when my basket will be filled.
My pockets may be empty, but still I'm basking in Gods Glory,
My life will be used one day to tell a great story.

My shoes may be tattered and worn, but it is just until,
I will not be in want for long, that's not my father's will.
I may look tired and weary; I have climbed many hills,
But I will reach the pinnacle, my blessings will come still.

My friends may reject me, I'm a prey left to be killed,
I may have to flee for safety, but it is just until.
In life I find no comfort, in life I find no peace,
But there will come a time when all this pain will cease.

Until then I will sing a glorious song,
Until then, by God's grace I will press on,
Until then, I'm resting in His arms where I belong,
Until then, just until then, with joy I will carry on.

Go to the Ant

Go to the ant you sluggard and consider its ways,
It collects its food in the summer time and stores for the winter days.
Go to the ant you sluggard; from it you may take a page,
It is always hard at work, it never procrastinates.

Wherever there is work, the ant finds it to do,
And wherever you see one, look out for number two.
The ant rarely sleeps; it is always on the move,
It knows too well that if it works hard, it has more to gain than to lose.

The ant has a vibrant team spirit, they work together well,
Their unity is their strength—on their differences they do not dwell.
The ant is a discipline insect; just look how coordinated they are,
They march to and from their harvest, whether it is near or far.

They live peacefully in their colonies; they work in one accord,
It is a social insect; team work wins them great rewards.
The ant is such a tiny insect; they carry very tiny feet,
They are not limited by their size, many obstacles they defeat.

They don't complain about their duties, they lift twenty times their weight,
They are very industrious insects, their own wealth they create.
Go to the ant you sluggard, to it you must try and relate,
From it you can learn lessons that will help you to be great.

Education

Education is a ladder that can carry us to greatness,
It is one of the keys that unlock doors to great success.
Education is the gateway to a bright and prosperous future,
It is not limited to race, colour, status or culture.

Education is not just about higher studying or getting high marks,
It's about learning all you can about a particular task.
Education is about discovering new things and increasing knowledge,
Obtaining education will certainly be to your best advantage.

Education helps you to work in a more organized and competent way,
Achieving maximum productivity and efficiency day by day.
Education forms the essence of what you say or do,
Your actions are influenced by what you know—they define you.

Education is self-empowerment, self-empowerment is power,
Knowledge can be the amplifier that shapes and electrifies your character.
Education better enables you to contribute to the growth of the nation,
It increases your earning power and ensures a firm financial foundation.

Try to increase knowledge every day; the ability to learn doesn't stop.
Always remember that "an idle mind is the devil's workshop."
An educated person who is influenced by Christ,
Will no doubt climb to the highest height.

Perfect Imperfections

Don't try to perfect your imperfections, or move from bad to worse,
Don't become an expert at making others curse.
Sometimes we are determined to be the worst that we can be,
Being strongly motivated when the tears of others we see.

Try not to feed of the pain of others or purposefully cause hurt,
Don't crush another's feelings, as if it quenches your egocentric thirst.
Be careful of the meek and humble who your actions bring to tears,
They might be the one who will help you unload your burdens and cares.

Oppression is a curse that raises its ugly head without us even knowing,
We need to be careful of the bad seeds that in our garden we are sowing.
When the day of harvest comes and it's our time to reap,
The sour grapes we feverishly sow might end up making us weep.

Imperfection is in our nature, we are sinful carnal beings,
But we were created with the ability to love with all our might and means.
Try to find the goodness that's hidden inside our heart,
The part of us that is willing to make the right start.

Recovery

Recovered my soul in the lost and found,
I'm on a new path I'm homeward bound.
This crazy road isn't easy; it is rather hard,
I have to make so many choices; have to play the right cards.

Home seems so near, yet still it is far,
Battles after battles, I can't seem to win this war.
The line is incredibly thin between happiness and sorrow,
Today you are smiling, you don't know about tomorrow.

It's difficult to do good; it takes no effort to do bad,
It's hard to control my anger; it's so easy to get mad.
I invest so much in happiness, so why am I in mourning,
Despair, weak and hopeless; some heavy loads I'm carrying

Many dark days behind me, some cloudy days ahead,
They say it's a highway to recovery, but don't you be misled.
Remember where I'm coming from, I was dead back then,
But I've got to show my strength, even when death threatens again.

So many hurts in life, too many reasons to cry,
Disappointments follow each other; I've deleted the word try.
My heart is filled with tears, but none flows from my eyes
I'm searching frantically for home, but it's nowhere in sight.

My load is getting heavier; my pains are getting sharper,
The pile of burden on my head is mounting up higher.
I'm walking through fire but I hope I'll get my heart's satisfaction,
In order to find home I need to steer in the right direction.

Actions and Reactions

Any where there is fire there is going to be some heat,
If you hit the rewind button, expect to see things repeat.
If you go to battle unprepared, expect to face a lost,
Remember everything in life comes at a cost.

If you plant a seed expect it to grow,
Don't open your palms if you have nothing to show.
If you press pause don't wait for things to go,
You can live life one of two ways, either fast or slow.

There's never an opening without a closing, or a beginning without an end,
Every first has a last and every one must lose a friend.
Don't expect summer to come just before winter, or autumn right before spring,
Your bird will never start barking, nor will your dog ever sing.

Every action brings a reaction; there are consequences for everything we do,
The consequences have great impact, they will affect you.
Where there's a start there's a finish, whatever you do expect an end result,
Bare these in mind and your life will be less difficult.

Fix Your Roof

Rain on the roof top creating melodies in my head,
Leak from the roof filling the faithful pot on my bed.
Loving the relaxing feeling, but I wish the rain would stop,
Because my pot keeps filling with every single rain drop.

Dreams, Hopes & Aspirations

It is a popular belief that life is hard and then you die,
And your spirit somehow is raised somewhere above the sky.
But you and I both know that many beliefs are not true,
Whether you are an optimist or a pessimist, your belief is up to you.

Life after death is a mystery to every single man,
Therefore live your life before death as best as you possibly can.
Work hard while you can, so when you can't life won't be hard,
And that will make all the myths stored in your head easier to discard.

Some aspects of life are inevitable, unavoidable they are,
Some will mend deep wounds, while some will create great scars.
So if your roof leaks don't blame the falling rain,
Precipitation is a must, but the faulty roof you can contain.

Fix the holes that you have, they'll surely make your life better,
Preparation is the key to weather life's stormy weather.
So live today well, so tomorrow can be great,
Life is for living, but remember, the inevitable we cannot escape.

My Shoes

Before you cast judgment
.........think about my shoe,
Don't form perceptions of me
.........until you take a look at my shoe,
Before you criticize me
.........reach out and touch my shoe,
If I fail to impress you
.........put just one foot in my shoe,
Before you under estimate me
.........slide both feet in my shoe,
And if you still doubt me
.........take just one step in my shoe,
Before you crucify me
.........walk a mile in my shoe,

You will better understand me
........when you run a day in my shoe,
Have you changed your perception
........now that you have felt my shoe?
My question to you is
........do you want to take my shoe?

The FIFA Giant

They are on the field without their stars Silva or Neymar,
Determined to remind the world just how great they are.
Being carefully watched by over two hundred million fans,
With nervous book keepers shivering in the stands.

This promises to be an exciting football match,
Samson vs. Goliath, this is a must watch.
Two of the world's greatest armed and ready to fight,
Another page of history will be written in front our sight.

Which one of these giants will be the first to fall?
These twenty two pairs of eye are fixed on one soccer ball.
This semi-final match of the 2014 world cup
Will see these two giants battling to reach the top.

Anthems are sung, camera light flashes from the crowd,
The kick off whistle is blown and the cheers from fans grow loud.
The first ten minutes is an exciting, impressive one,
But the Brazilians took their eyes off one German.

A corner is taken and Muller is left without a mark,
He plunges the ball in the net like a hungry shark.
From there it was a downward spiral for the host team,
Sealing German's faith, destroying Brazil's dream.

One by one the ball finds the back of the Brazilians net,
Scolari on the sideline soaking in fretful sweat.

Dreams, Hopes & Aspirations

One giant is becoming weak; it's falling to the ground,
Seven goals to nil and the Brazilian fans make not a sound.

Two hundred million fans look in frantic disbelief,
A humiliated coach Luiz Scolari sobs in extreme grief.
Eleven men in red and black enjoying the taste of victory,
Eleven men in yellow and green mourning bitterly.

The last thirty seconds just before the final whistle blows,
Oscar desperately plunges one in German's net to end the show.
But the great giant stumbles, a new hero has emerged,
Seven goals to one, Brazil's ego has submerged.

Described as the greatest defeat in Brazil's football history,
Their 39 years unbeaten record at home was tarnished by Germany.
This historical day will forever be remembered,
July 8, 2014, when the Brazilian gods were brutally slaughtered.

Four days after defeat, the dead giants have a chance to resurrect,
They have much to prove, many mistakes to correct.
Their captain, Silva, has now joined the pack,
They are about to show the world that the giants are back.

Just minutes in the game and they are under attack,
Goal number 1, 2, 3, and Brazil's grey clouds turn black.
The stadium in Brasilia echoes with deafening boos,
No redemption for Brazil, once again they lose.

Slaughtered by the German's, buried by the Dutch,
Their dreams are now a nightmare, all hopes have being crushed.
If they recover by 2018, they can try to reclaim the crown,
But I'm sure the Germans and the Dutch will be there to slow them down.

*Here
&
Now*

Time

Consider yourself lucky if time stays by your side,
Many have tried to hold on to it, but with them it wouldn't abide.
Time waits on no one, it moves at its own pace,
So if it lingers for a while, make haste! You don't have much to waste.

Time is very precious; it cannot be bought or sold,
It doesn't matter if you possess the finest or rarest gold.
It places the rich and the poor on a level ground,
Where many differences exists, but just one similarity is found.

Time has taught us an important lesson; the present is the best,
The 'now' is the opportune moment, the closest to anything perfect.
Don't wait until tomorrow, procrastination and time aren't friends,
'Time' and 'now' walk hand in hand; better 'now' than 'then.'

So waste no time, the setting of the sun is near,
Do all that you have to do while the skies are clear.
Whether it moves slowly, or whether it's in haste,
Time is an unbeatable element, with it you cannot race.

Age

If I had known I would have taken your advice,
Instead I allowed it to overtake me by surprise.
It crept up on me like a thief in the night,
It gave me a scare, it gave me a fright.

You knew quite well it would have come my way,
You warned me about that terrible day,
When wrinkles would come and grey hair would appear,
And the youth in my face would suddenly disappear.

How shall I escape this thing called age?
I'm trying to comprehend how I've reached this stage,

I was once a man of valour, now I'm weak and frail,
I am like an old train that's about to derail.

Time has caught up with me; I can no longer do the miles,
It has robbed me of my boyish looks and my wrinkle free smile.
I was once agile as a gymnast; I was nimble as a deer
Now the vigour and vitality in me has slowly disappeared.

My limbs are becoming whimpish, my body is frail and weak,
I am no longer robust; I can't find the strength I seek.
Years have overtaken me; my eyes aren't bright as before,
No longer can I thread a needle, my sight has gotten poor.

The truth is I miss my youth and I fear what's ahead,
I am scared about getting old, I rather stay young instead.
My vim, vigour and vitality once made me a well favoured man,
Now I just reminisce on the past, trying to survive as long as I can.

Live your youthful life to the fullest; enjoy it while it last,
Do all the things you possibly can, because age will come real fast.
Make many happy memories, you'll need them in a few,
As long as you can, do everything you are able to do.

Generation of Nothing

Morals degraded, sacred laws desecrated,
Values downgraded, society insulted,
Love and hate related, values and positive attitudes separated,
Violence and peace integrated, law and order mutilated.

A generation of vipers, scaring society beyond recognition,
Destroying the legacy of our faithful forefathers' actions.
Hard work is like leprosy, laziness now the new favoured occupation,
Grand theft and other illegals are now targeted professions.

Freedom of speech and other expressions been taken too far,
One of the reason the true meaning of a family is now marred.

For children to access sexually explicit materials is far from hard,
Morality and ethical behavior humans disregard.

Idleness and laziness is now a part of our cultural design,
Instead of seeing them as destructive factors, we justify these parasitic vines.
Generation of insolence, deteriorating society at the speed of light,
A generation in utter darkness; this our woeful plight.

A generation of insanity, generation of inhumanity,
A generation of demoniacs bringing about maniacal frenzy.
A generation of education, generation of technology,
A generation tricked with physical freedom, but trapped by mental slavery.

Alcohol's Claws

The Claws of Alcohol leaves a nasty Scar,
An enemy of humanity that is trying effortlessly to win this war.
It swirls around smoothly then bites like a snake,
Causing wrong things to be done; wrong decisions to be made.

Wine is a mocker, strong drink is raging,
It stings like a viper, you won't know until you start aching.
This silent killer leads to overbearing insolence and chaos,
Creating widespread mayhem, not just for addicts, but for all of us.

One of man's worst enemies—destroying lives is its mission,
Creating a path of destruction with its spiteful addiction.
It becomes your kryptonite; you'll never be the same,
The only thing it guarantees is disgrace, death and shame.

That one bottle could take you down a dreadful and regrettable path,
Slowly seducing you then unleashing its angry wrath.
Alcohol's addiction; a long hard battle to fight,
One sip—one taste—could turn your sunny days into stormy nights.

Time to Go

You have taken me through many sleepless nights and many tested days,
You have seen my many fights; I'm a slave to my ignorant ways.
You have stood beside me while I aimlessly moved to and fro,
But today my faithful friend is the day that you must go.

I have told you all my fears; all my secrets you know,
You have drowned out my sorrows, but you have made my thinking slow.
You have numbed my heart to all life's terrible hurt and pains,
I'll miss you my friend, without you I would have gone insane.

You took your place in my life when I needed you there the most,
You've helped me to smile, masking my scariest inner ghost.
Sometimes you would knock me down harder than you should,
But I accepted your whipping because I know your intentions were good.

I stare at you with sadness old friend, but I will refill you no more,
I'll wash you and lock you away behind the cupboard door.
I'll miss our nights together, you surely kept me warm,
But retiring from consuming you, will do me more good than harm.

Please don't try to seduce me; I'll never come back to you,
Some unions were not meant to be, which includes our union too.
Good bye my dear old whisky, I'm sorry but I must move on,
It's very hard for me to do, but to you I must say so long.

Drugs

It enters your life gently,
Fixes your problems temporarily,
Gets you addicted slowly,
Reassures you calmly,
Tricks you speedily,
Turns your life into hell bitterly,
Destroys you silently,
Humiliates you publicly.

It leaves you hopeless,
Your mouth becomes toothless,
Your life becomes meaningless,
It leaves you jobless,
Hungry because you are penniless,
Cold because you are homeless,
Lonely because you are friendless,
And soon you become lifeless.

Be careful of drugs it turns you into waste,
No matter what form, colour, state or taste.
Don't become a part of the statistic of another helpless case,
Remember that you are not immune no matter your age or race.
It doesn't choose its victims based on complexion of the face,
Just one little try and your whole life can be erased.
Let's fight against drugs and let's do it in a haste.

Different Me

Same old you, looking at a different me,
Changed by life's harsh lessons, now I can clearly see.
Time wasting days are over, serious times are here,
Life doesn't grant us pardon, all my anguish I must bear.

If you want to reach me you will have to climb very high,
My intentions are great; my confidence has pushed my limit to the sky.
I'm on a different level, I am standing tall,
I am determined to move upwards and I don't intend to fall.

Regression is my enemy, I embrace progress,
My cup will soon be filled; I'll soon have much success.
I refuse to believe that I'm running an unwinnable race,
I may not be at the front, but I'm certainly not in last place.

The old me would have remained complacent,
The new me is persistent, much to my amazement,
No longer just existing, the new me is actually living,
I'm growing stronger, loving more, achieving much and thriving.

Moral Trauma

The reality is that we are faced with a moral and social trauma,
Where doing right is an enigma, and doing wrong is on people's agenda.
Infidelity is the norm and loyalty comes with an expiration date,
The only love some persons know is just to love to hate.

Honesty and integrity are held with scant regard,
They are viewed as outdated values that offer no rewards.
They are forbidden grounds that are no longer trotted by man,
These moral values people no longer try to understand.

Darkness and licentiousness casts a gloom over life,
Any form of dignity that was left we have sacrificed.
The deterioration of human behavior has caused society to lose its worth,
But to a new moral culture we need to give birth.

Ethics should be promoted, immorality demoted,
Positive values uplifted, negative attitudes downgraded,
Human rights respected; this should be the direction of our new path,
Where morals and values are things that will eternally last.

I am Suicide

They testify that it gives them thrills,
But I certify that smoking kills.
You are explicitly warned that it's a leading cause of death,
With each puff, you take away your own breath.

That cool, refreshing feeling that goes up to your brain,
Which lifts you ten feet high, will actually cause long term pain.
Outside it's a stick of tobacco, in your body it's like dynamite,
With this there's no need for hindsight, all you need is foresight.

Bear in mind that your addiction doesn't only affect you,
Innocent lives are torn apart simply by the things you do.

Second hand smoking is dangerous to others health,
From it we get sick too, and that certainly diminishes our wealth.

Smoking kills! Doesn't that give you the chills?
They're leaving you to commit suicide at your own free will.
You can clearly see the danger of the choice that you make,
And the only time some persons stop is when it's just too late...

So the next time you take up that dynamite and that light,
Think about whether the choice that you make is wrong or if it's alright.
Fight the addiction, you can quit still.
Remember that both first hand and second hand smoking painfully kills.

Stony Land

I stay in stony land; there my happiness increase,
No pain, no hurt, no care, no fear, no grief, just peace.
I stay in stony land, a place where dreams are real,
A place where all brokenness gets a chance to heal.

In stony land I am the star of a one man show,
All the tactics to survive in this life I know.
I am a legend, a hero, a very mighty one,
I am less than a God, but greater than a man.

In stony land I have real friends,
Friends who my honor they will gladly defend.
Friends who treat me like I deserve,
Friends who do not use me only as a reserve.

I stay in stony land because there I am complete,
All the troubles of life seem to be obsolete.
The worries and cares I leave them at the gate,
You can create your own stony land, it's never too late.

Just sit back, relax, and allow your imagination to run wild,
Fantasies weren't only made for a child.

Put a smile on your face and bask in your freedom of thoughts,
Create your stony land, it can't be sold, it can't be bought.

Nothing

Here today, gone tomorrow,
This life isn't ours, it's only borrowed.
What is man that you should be mindful of him?
We are like the chaff that blows in the wind.

We are beautiful well-groomed flowers,
That blooms gracefully in the springtime and dies after summer.
We came from dust; back to dust we shall go,
Some will go very fast, some will go very slow.

Why do we boast of riches and earthly possessions?
We treasure vanity that points us in hells direction.
Our carnal being is prone to sin,
We are fighting a war that by ourselves we cannot win.

So to no man, feel yourself above or beneath,
We came here with nothing, and that's how we'll go underneath.
Our light shines bright today, tomorrow they might go dim,
We are encouraged to live happily and find peace within.

Peaceful Sleep

There she was sleeping peacefully like a babe,
Eyes shut tight, no reason to be afraid.
No troubling thoughts, no worries, no cares,
Not a heavy load to carry, not a burden to bear.

From this miserable world she has escaped,
Now she's on her way to a peaceful grave.

There she'll rest in peace no one to contend with,
Having no temptations to try and resist.

She slept as we wept, having no emotions to show,
Leaving everything behind, going empty handed below.
I hope she'll rest in peace, but we will never know,
Her time is now; it'll soon be our time to go.

It's great to be alive but death shouldn't be feared,
It's an episode that's inevitable so don't be scared.
Live life to the fullest, love much, and laugh more,
Soon you won't be able to enjoy them anymore.

It will be us who will be sporting a straight face,
Awaiting pallbearers to bring us to our grave.
Six feet deep, the final resting place,
From the cold hands of death no one is safe.

Rain Amidst Sunshine

Rain amidst sunshine, tears amidst joy,
Smiles hide the pains, there's nothing to enjoy.
A rose enjoys the daylight, but bow its head at nights,
I wonder if in the dark it is a less than beautiful sight.

I too am happy on the outside, and everyone can see,
The beauty of God's creation is really shown on me.
But inside I am fighting a battle of agony and pain,
So behind this sunshine smile, is a life that's bitterly stained.

O yes, I've had my good times, life wasn't always sad,
The skies were sometimes clear; I was left feeling quite glad.
Happiness was very evident, laughter highlighted my days,
My burdens seemed extremely light, and I found much joy in giving praise.

Oh happiness, where art thou, please show thyself once more,
I know, for me, thou hast many bright days and peaceful nights in store.

So don't think that I'm ungrateful, I remain resolute to my faith,
I am very optimistic, my turn around will be great.

Technology

We live in large developed cities, technology at its peak,
The world has become a global village, everything becomes unique.
But with all the modern technology and amazing breakthrough in science,
The question that I ask is, "Are we civilized?"

We spend hours on Facebook, chatting to strangers that we'll never meet,
But we ignore the person sitting beside us on the same bus seat.
We follow celebrities on Twitter further increasing their fame,
But we stay away from our neighbours; we don't even try to know their name.

We search for partners on dating websites, we select them carefully,
When there are virtuous women in our reach who we ignore totally.
We play games on the internet with persons thousands of miles away,
But cannot play with our siblings for ten minutes out of the day.

Our smart phone is our life, this gadget we can't do without,
It is like our sixth sense, we carry it all about.
These phones are incredible, but we use them more than our brains,
We depend on them so much that without them we would go insane.

Playgrounds are empty, no more playing on the side street,
No group of friends chilling on park benches, listening to rappers beat.
We become ghosts to each other; technology is to be blamed,
Resulting in little human interaction, our social skills have become maimed.

We take a giant step forward; technology has created a revolution,
We have seen for ourselves this tremendous evolution.
But with such great power, have we proven to be wise?
We take few steps backwards, so are we civilized?

Dark Era

Another dark era in the history of man,
We have had so much violence sweeping our land.
Weapons of mass destruction wiping out innocent lives,
They have left fatherless children and husbandless wives.

So many harmless beings struggling to survive,
We see many broken families trying to be revived.
Too many mass murders, too many mass graves,
Too many lost souls that are waiting to be saved.

The gun has become one of man's best friends,
A weapon full of wrath that has cut many lives to an end.
Heartless beasts ripping decent lives apart,
As one saga ends, another saga starts.

There are lovers killing lovers in jealous, destructive rage,
We see babies having babies at a very tender age.
Man has taken one step forward but we jump backwards twice,
We think we are geniuses but we are very unwise.

Technology at its peak has created a great revolution,
But we use it selfishly to our own destruction.
Man! We have become our own worst enemy,
We fail to understand the concept of togetherness and harmony.

As intelligent as we are, we are so confused,
Life should be a great win, but we still chose to lose.
We are defeated by ignorance; we are defeated by greed,
We are defeated by life because of our villainous deeds.

But it's time to rise and make a change; this is our fight,
Let's change our ending, turn a new page and do things right.
We have reached a stage where we cannot compromise,
We simply need to join together, it's worth the sacrifice.

Never Felt My Pain

How can you understand me if you have never felt my pain,
There are not enough words for me to ever explain.
Again … I ask you not to sympathize,
It gives me no comfort if you are not able to empathize.

My fears are real, my tears concealed,
My anger suppressed, I'm emotionally distressed.
Life is seeking redress for all the troubles I have caused,
While I make no claims for everything I have lost.

How can you say you feel my pain?
You have never experienced agonies that are driving me insane.
Have you ever cried bitterly but your tears are ignored?
Or bruised your knees from kneeling but you still don't feel reassured?

Have you ever pleaded for someone to listen to your cause?
But they totally ignore you just because of who you are?
You can try and relate to the things that I say,
But you will never comprehend them in the same way.

I look forward to the day when the skies won't be grey,
When good fortune will come and misfortune will be delayed,
When all agonies will ease and torments will cease,
When despair will disappear and I'll experience peace.

I await my day of jubilee when all sorrows will be gone,
The old me shall pass and a new me shall be reborn,
But for now trials and tribulations still exists.
In my present life I am hoping for an amazing twist.

Overdue

I'm tired of listening because I don't hear the answer,
I unclasp my hands because of too many unanswered prayers.

Here & Now

How can I count my blessings when my poor heart aches?
Where there should be happiness there's a huge empty space.

I wonder if it's possible to speak the love language,
When my heart, body and soul is in trapped in hates bondage.
This once perfect smile has lost all its meaning,
Happiness is something that exists only when I'm dreaming.

My stares are frigid; they're like the South Pole,
They carry no warm feeling, they're brutally cold.
I hope I'm not selfish; I'm just trying to figure it all out,
Wondering if at some point there will be a turnabout.

I don't mean any disrespect to my maker and my king,
Who has the power to cleanse me from outside and within.
But I really have to wonder have you forgotten about me?
I'm the same guy who you promised to show pity and mercy.

One more time I ask you not to pass me by,
Lord, I know that you see these tears that I cry.
Lord, just in case my unanswered prayers are in the cue,
I'll wait patiently even though my happiness is long overdue.

Confused

Afraid to live but scared to die,
I look up to the sky and ask God why.
Why aren't my prayers been answered?
Why does it seem like my name you don't remember?
Why after I pray I end up crying longer?
Why after I read my Bible I end up feeling weaker?

I smile to hide my fear; laugh to hide my pain,
I feel so alone, getting beaten by the rain.
The sun comes out in its glory but doesn't shine my way,
Depression and discouragement have my mind in disarray.
I desperately question God night after night, day after day.

There is pain in my words, angry lyrics in my head,
Don't need to try living, when I'm already dead.
I've made my own thorns, put them in my own bed,
Then I lay me down to sleep, closing my eyes in content.

I drown myself with tears; I force myself to sleep,
I avoid been awake so I don't have to weep,
But before I close my eyes I pray the Lord my soul to keep.

Even if I fail to wake, I know I'll rest in peace.
My burdens, my cares, my torments will cease.

And when I resurrect, His face I will see.

Life Cycle of a Hustler

Fathers dodging prison while their sons are dying,
They are nowhere around to wipe the tears of hurtful mothers crying.
These men become statistics; they are placed on the wall of shame,
So many mothers left behind, having to bear the pain.

Boys are falling behind while girls are impressively excelling,
Some don't even care that low achievements make them less appealing.
To many misguided young men life is just a game,
Is it nature or nurture, where do we cast the blame?

No longer do boys dream about joining a recognized profession,
They are not willing to work and climb the ladder of success in
    any organization.
Instead quick money, power and easy life is their goal,
For this they will sacrifice their lives, they will even sell their souls.

They seem to forget the saying, 'easy come, easy go'
To hustling they say yes, to hard work they say no.
The boys become men with no moral values or vision,
Their life style and reality now caught up in a head on collision.

These boys become fathers, dodging prison and life behind bars,
They thought they took the easy way out, now life becomes hard,
They leave children with no fatherly guidance or fatherly supervision.
Boys without dreams become men without vision, having no one to guide them in the right direction …

Midnight's Cry

If I had a choice, I would choose not to be so common,
Here, there, everywhere, moving from hand to hand.
I was being picked up by men of all races,
Handled like a doll, staring in strange faces.

I changed location as I changed my clothes,
Eating meals in a married man's home.
Now I'm sharing a bed with a man and his wife,
Under her pillow is a sharp kitchen knife,

She's waiting for midnight to snatch his breath,
Could I be the reason he's marked for death?
My mother was this married man's lover,
I am the 4 month old product of them being together.

Did daddy tell his wife, I wonder how does she know?
No one is here to stay, at midnight daddy will go.
Now there's a mother on the go, a wife on the run,
A cheating husband in the morgue and a fatherless son.

In the Streets

There I was lying on the vicious street,
I felt so weak I just couldn't use my feet.
I struggled with myself trying to take a stand,
But you passed me by without giving me a hand.

You saw me outside curled up, freezing in the cold,
The garment I had on was rugged, thin and very old.
You didn't offer me a blanket or a jacket to keep me warm,
Or even a temporary shelter just to weather the storm.

You saw me sitting alone with tears flowing from my eyes,
My pleas for help were loud; you heard my desperate cries,
You slowly looked away and didn't ask me what was wrong,
You simply walked by, humming your sweet little song.

I was sweaty, smelly and dirty, I didn't shower for a while,
But even though you frowned at me I bravely held my smile.
You covered your nose and passed me, you looked at me with scorn,
I was treated as if I was the worst thing that was ever born.

It was on your way to church on that beautiful Christmas day,
I was feeling quite ill when I helplessly stumbled in your way.
I was quite shock when I heard the words you had to say,
Those distasteful words came from your mouth that you will use to pray.

You sing on the church choir, you sometimes preach too,
The things that you say in church are the things you fail to do.
You are a hypocrite and a pretender; you do not practice what you teach,
But if you teach the right and do the wrong, heaven you will not reach.

Heartless – Mindless

My mind has no heart; my heart has no brain,
That is why my actions cause so much pain.
I act with no heart,
I love with no thought,
My heartless mind deceives,
My mindless heart intrigues.

My outer joy shines, my inner pain it conceals,
Fearing that one day the true me will be revealed.
My words are sharp, they cut like razor,

My calm appearance masks my anger.
There is this illusion that pain makes you stronger,
So why does my heart, mind and body feel weaker?

My mindless heart made me believe I was a lover,
But my heartless mind screams "you are a hater."
But I won't listen to you any longer,
I will not allow my heart or my mind to become an avenger.
I'll give my mind a heart and I'll give my heart a brain,
I won't allow heartless and brainless to drive me insane.

My Purpose

My life is empty, empty indeed,
My purpose in life I cannot see.
My burdens are heavy, my heart often weeps,
My purpose Lord is not clear to me.

My knees are bruised from kneeling low,
Praying to The Lord my purpose to show.
I need an answer, I need to know,
Lord show me my purpose so I can go.

I'm wretched and blind Lord, just dust I am,
I've wasted my life Lord following my own plan,
I've found no comfort; I'm still an empty man,
Lord what is my purpose, show me where to stand.

I'm out of options; I'm running out of time,
For the years I have are quickly slipping by.
I'm very confused Lord, I'm losing my mind,
My purpose in life Lord I need to find.

Beauty and the Beast

They call me beauty
But I am the beast.
My outwards is comely
My inner human deceased.

You see a perfect smile
But I feel the deepest pain.
My outside glows brightly,
Inside I am disdained.

My soul is full of scars
It makes me mortified,
I'm scared of my own weakness
My soul longs to be fortified.

My beauty is quite charming
My beast is not quite nice,
You see the outer me rejoicing
The inner me is cold as ice.

My beauty conflicts with my beast
One is full of fury, the other seeks peace.
Daily this struggle intensifies,
Now I realise the strength of my beast.

Poisoned Minds

We poison our minds with things that degrade us,
We do stupid things suggested by people who know nothing about us,
We are a part of every trend even though we know they're not for us,
My question is...When will we start doing things that truly define us?

We try every Facebook challenge even when they prove to be dangerous,
We sing every song on airplay no matter how outrageous,
We entertain conversations that to others are malicious,
My question is … Will we ever be a generation who takes life serious?

We need to remember that societal norms are set by us,
What we do influence the people around us,
When we do things wrong don't be afraid to correct us,
My question is … Will you be willing to stand by us?

It's ok to explore; our minds are naturally curious,
But we need to set boundaries in case we get delirious,
Our own actions bring reactions that make us furious,
The answer is clear … We are simply mysterious.

Hopeful Pain

My heart is in a desolate place,
It's sad, lonely and without grace.
The pride I once had is no longer there,
My joys are gone; I have no good cheer to share.

My heart is heavy with all of life's troubles,
All my happiness comes in singles, but my pains come in doubles.
This poor heart stands alone; it's filled with fears and doubts,
It screams but I hear nothing, no sounds run with my shouts.

My heart is faint and weak,
I search, I wander, but cannot find what I seek.
I stretch for joy but my heart's hands cannot reach,
But I'm trying real hard not to accept defeat.

My heart is still beating but I am so dead,
This soul should be at peace but it's miserable instead.
Many sorrows torment me like needles in my bed,
The voice of despair beat drums in my head.

With all these pains I'm reminded of a special love that exists,
The one that Christ has to offer; the one I cannot resist.
This love is what is keeping me to stand from day to day,
I know He'll ease my pain; for me He'll clear the way.

Appreciate It

It's during winter's cold that you eagerly anticipate summer's heat,
Having bitter experiences will leave you longing for something sweet.
Don't take your happy days for granted, there'll be days when you'll get sad,
Life won't always be good, so always prepare for the days that will be bad.

Cherish your youth; soon you'll get old,
The wrinkles on your skin will be bright and bold.
Don't forget the bottom even when you've reached the top,
It can hurt very badly when from the top you drop.

Don't complain about the night, just try and anticipate the day,
There's a reason God has blessed it with the sun's rays.
The mornings are a blessing; it comes with the rising of the sun,
The evenings bring an end to a day of toiling well done.

When life knocks us down we fight hard to get up,
Determined like an angry volcano waiting to erupt.
So appreciate every great moment as long as they last,
Tomorrow may not be as pleasing as the day that has past.

We invite you to view the complete
selection of titles we publish at:

www.ASPECTBooks.com

scan with your mobile
device to go directly
to our website

Please write or email us your praises, reactions, or
thoughts about this or any other book we publish at:

P.O. Box 954
Ringgold, GA 30736

Info@ASPECTBooks.com

TEACH Services, Inc., titles may be purchased in bulk for
educational, business, fund-raising, or sales promotional use.
For information, please e-mail:

BulkSales@ASPECTBooks.com

Finally if you are interested in seeing
your own book in print, please contact us at

publishing@ASPECTBooks.com

We would be happy to review your manuscript for free.

www.ingramcontent.com/pod-product-compliance
Lightning Source LLC
Chambersburg PA
CBHW070557160426
43199CB00014B/2535